MW01595629

Advance Praise for

"If you want to see honesty and authenticity, read this book. If you want to laugh, read this book. If you don't mind being challenged to stretch and grow, read this book. For me, reading this book was a painful look in the mirror and a breath of fresh air. After reading this book, I feel like I really know Steve—and I know myself better too."

—Keith Madison
National Baseball Director, SCORE International
Head Baseball Coach, University of Kentucky 1979-2003

"As conversational and simple as rocking and talking on a front porch with a friend, Steve Elder takes you to a place called change. He shows us the desire in each of us to live fully, love deeply and lead well the lives we are created to step into."

—Chip Dodd
Author, *The Voice of the Heart*
Executive Director, Center for Professional Excellence

"Steve Elder has a wonderful story to tell. Find a comfortable chair, a bright light, and be prepared to spend the next few hours being fully entertained and educated. Steve's story illustrates that one's life chart doesn't have to go north by northeast in order to be successful. Instead, by citing examples of his own life experience, Steve has shown that by looking at yourself in the mirror, and accepting the warts of one's life lessons, a person can find joyful, healthy, and energetic life."

—Lee Geiger
Managing Director, Penserra Securities
Writer of "The Daily Pundit"

"Steve uses his Southern charm and excellent storytelling ability to lightheartedly pose very serious questions. I found myself laughing, crying and reflecting on his thoughts over and over, even after I had finished the book."

—Christy Parsons
CEO, Dabora, Inc.

"Mixing humor in with serious lessons, Steve Elder does like the old preacher once said: to 'Hit 'em when they are laughing.' Steve offers insight into his soul in an effort to help his readers find what we all desire—joy. Real joy. And along with joy, we are given strength. Steve does an excellent job of describing how they work hand-in-hand. Before I read this book, I liked cornbread. I am sorry—I will never eat it again."

—Vincent Matlock
President, S.M. Lawrence Co., Inc.
Board of Directors, Comfort Systems, Inc.

"The wit and humor in this book is Steve Elder, a wonderful man who shares his journey in a thought provoking way. It will make you smile, laugh out loud, reflect and begin to look at your life in a different way. He guides you through questions that help walk you through your own story. A book written for anyone who wants to create change and movement, and live life to the fullest!"

—Joanne Ferguson
President, Advisor Pathways, Inc.

"Steve Elder writes with a gritty spirituality—honest, gutsy, and a humor in the style of the Lewis Grizzards of the world that keeps you engaged in the story. He invites you to join him on a spiritual pilgrimage that matches faith and life in the trenches of common struggle."

—Dr. Mark Gregory
Author, *Net Trigger*

"In this powerful book, Steve Elder uses the gift of humor to show us how our life experiences are the greatest teacher of all. You will view your relationship with yourself, as well as with others, in a new and exciting way."

—Chuck Pruett
Managing Partner, The Pruett Group,
Northwestern Mutual Financial Network

"*How Much More Longer?* is a thought provoking dose of life's realities sincerely. This book will prompt you to do some healthy self examination and reflection on life's priorities."

—Jim Allen
CEO, Hilliard Lyons

"Steve Elder writes with such 'down to earth' candor that you get caught up in his story. Then you realize it is not so different from yours. His humorous, introspective and honest approach is refreshing and challenging. We need men who will be honest about their humanity. Men who aren't afraid to laugh at themselves and talk about their mistakes and the lessons learned. Steve is one of those guys, and he speaks the refreshing language of an authentic heart in a way that invites you right in—to his story and yours."

—Russ Lee
Recording Artist, Lead Singer, Newsong

"Life's too short to learn everything the hard way. This book will shorten your learning curve."

—Brady Cooper
Pastor, New Vision Church

"After learning Steve Elder had actually written a book, I could only come to one conclusion. We are hours from damnation."

—Steve's High School English teacher

HOW MUCH MORE LONGER?

HOW

MUCH

MORE

LONGER?

STEVE ELDER

HOW TO GET REAL NOW ABOUT LIVING THE LIFE YOU WANT

Pleasant Word (a division of WinePress Publishing, PO Box 428, Enumclaw, WA 98022) functions only as book publisher. As such, the ultimate design, content, editorial accuracy, and views expressed or implied in this work are those of the author.

ISBN 13: 978-1-4141-1477-4
ISBN 10: 1-4141-1477-X
Library of Congress Catalog Card Number: 2009904482

This book is dedicated to Vicki, Ashley and Ben.
Only when we get to heaven will you know
the love my heart carries for you.

Twenty years from now you will be more disappointed by the things that you didn't do than by the ones you did do. So throw off the bowlines. Sail away from the safe harbor. Catch the trade winds in your sails. Explore. Dream. Discover.

—attributed to Mark Twain

CONTENTS

PREFACE

MY FORTY-THREE YEARS have been eventful. From surviving a right-at-death experience, to sharing with thousands of people through my business or talks I have given, I have lived out my own journey while also listening to others share their struggles and victories. Everyone has such a unique story to tell, and too often those stories go untold, even to those closest to them.

I have noticed some common things that we all seem to share. We believe our private struggles are made to be . . . well, private. We think no one cares or that people would judge us, or that folks might not think so highly of us if they knew the real me and what I was *really* thinking.

But the problem is . . . those folks are often thinking the same thing. Those people sitting beside you at dinner? They are going through the same sort of struggles you are. When people get permission to communicate authentically, it is amazing how fast walls come down and true relationships are formed. And if there is one thing we are missing in our families, our neighborhoods, our churches, and our workplaces, it is community. The feeling, no, the knowledge, of knowing there are people locked in with us, helping us to live our lives in a way that is conscious, real and full of freedom.

We also share a sense of aimlessness, a drifting. Oh, we are awake to our careers some of the time, and we hear what our children say occasionally, but we are so dazed and confused by the haze of activity that surrounds us like dense fog that we are merely trying to get to the next thing, whatever that may be. In the process, we lose ourselves, our purpose, our dreams. As a result, we are present a *lot*, but we aren't really there. We aren't engaged. We haven't grabbed our purpose and our heart, hanging onto it like our life and our living depended on it.

And it does.

My experience says that a lot of people would not guess that about you. You might have picked up some trophies or awards along the way, shown everyone how successful you are, just how together you have it. But once I have gotten to know someone and hear all of their story, I have found out that no one like that exists, and the pressures we put on ourselves to give that aura are just mind-numbingly exhausting.

My son Ben used to sit in his car seat in the back. Any time we took a trip he deemed long, say over six minutes, he would sit holding his sippy cup and stare into the rearview mirror and say, "How much more longer, Daddy?"

And that is what I aim to ask you in the following pages, through my story and some questions I have about yours.

How much more longer are you going to go on living this way? How much more longer are you going to live with an unfulfilled promise, with the shadows of dreams that you think are simply out of reach or that you have given up on? How much longer will you go on living for hollow purposes, with goals that are not even yours, goals that are someone else's agenda instead of your own?

Come along. I invite you to my story.

I bet you find yours, too.

—Steve Elder

INTRODUCTION

DON'T LET THE tone or title of this book fool you.
While I hope the stories in it make you smile, its messages
are serious ones. I believe in something my grandfather, Pop, used
to say: "You catch more flies with honey than with vinegar." That's
why when penicillin tastes like bubble gum or grape Kool-Aid, it's
easier to give it to your kids. But the penicillin has a serious job
to do.

Mostly, this book is a collection of my stories about growing
up in the South and the humor that, by definition, comes with
that territory. Do you remember Steve Martin's alter ego Navin
Johnson's opening line, "I was born a poor black boy. . . " from the
1979 movie *The Jerk*? That line is a classic example of the kind of
humor that is intended here. If you don't get that kind of humor or
are offended by it, I make two guesses about you: perhaps you have
never learned to laugh at yourself, or maybe you had your funny
bone removed shortly after birth. I'm going to try to reattach it.

Life does have a way of offering us a humorous lens through
which we can view the events that make up our lives. For me, and
I hope for you, humor gives us moments that beg serious thought
as we observe the way we humans act, react, and generally screw

it all up. I count myself among those souls who have never quite figured life out, but who are making the honest effort to do so.

Serious events have pierced my world on more than one occasion, and I attempt to weave those through this story. My recollections are my own, seen through my lens, and they are unique to me. But writing my story has opened me to the reality that we all have a story. Some stories are more painful or memorable than others, but they are our own one-of-a-kind quilt nonetheless.

There was a time in my life when I worked, came home, and had two questions. One, What are we eatin'? Next, When does the next *Sportscenter* come on? I wasn't thinkin' about nothin'.

The simple reason I began this book was selfish. I wanted my story on paper for my children, and I was struck by how many people purport to know me well that do not have the whole story. But a larger issue took hold of me as I began to remember and write about my forty-three years.

We walk around largely without two things that are essential to life: meaningful, conscious thought and laughter. The times are admittedly serious ones—but they have made us so serious that joy is nothing more than a concept. The very things that were supposed to free us up—technology, the ability to telecommute, cell phones, the Internet, these things and others—have served to make us. . .noisy. Busy. Efficient.

Maybe. . .but we're a lot less happy and fulfilled. "Breaking news" is everywhere. Information is at our fingertips. Communication—or "keeping tabs"—is instantaneous, changing the way we date, parent, manage, and allow stress to swallow us up, never stopping to *think*. We have choices—yet we have allowed the noise of 10,000 songs in our pocket and various other competing demands to crowd into and control our thoughts and our actions. Everything is urgent. I have to-do lists which include doing my other to-do lists.

Mostly, we frown.

And that's not what makes life fun. I've watched some of those frowns disappear as folks have laughed at my stories, and I have been urged on more than one occasion to put my "sick" mind to work sharing how I see the world.

I draw on a couple of things that have taken up a good share of my adult life. I have worked in the financial services business and run my own wealth advisory practice for the last twenty years, hearing fears, hopes, victories, dreams, and frustrations expressed in equal measure from my clients and friends. I have spoken to many individuals and led community groups for the last decade. Combine those experiences with raising a couple of children into teenagers and you have yourself quite the experience cocktail. I am honored to have traveled with so many in about every facet of life, and I hope the stories of many of these people shine through clearly. But the experience of other people is not your story, nor is it mine.

Yet I do believe we can learn from each other. Sometimes we learn the hard way. If you stumble across a sentence or a paragraph in this book and think you detect pain and humility, it is because you do. My heart is so full. I want to share my experiences with you and I hope you are blessed by the effort. It is my privilege to share them, hard earned as they may have been.

Now, come with me. Let's peel the years back and look at what the world done gone and done.

CHAPTER 1

HELLO, PAIN—YOU SUCK

Pain is temporary. It may last a minute, or an hour, or a day, or a year, but eventually it will subside and something else will take its place. If I quit, however, it lasts forever.

—Lance Armstrong

THE FIRST THING I saw was Michelle.

The next thing we both saw was my left index finger, hanging by a strand of skin.

What I did not know was that my new stubby friend was the least of my immediate concerns.

July 9, 1984. The setting was a perfect summer night. I left the country baseball park after watching a couple of games—I didn't play that night, though I did have practice. My teammate Randy asked for a ride out to see friends play because his car was broken down and I was taking him home. Tough break for Randy, as you will see. . . .

I was driving on a small rural road when my little Honda Accord met up with a 1975 Chevelle driven by a drunk driver. In the clash between the two cars, my Honda lost the fight. My passenger and baseball teammate Randy and I awoke to a new reality. Innocence was gone, along with all sensation throughout our bodies. That

1

turned out to be a temporary but welcome reprieve from what was about to become my new teacher—pain.

To that point, my life had been a Wonder World of childhood bliss. My family affectionately called our home "Elder Mountain," though the illusion of a mountain was only because my grandparents lived at road level and our house sat in a flood area about twenty-five feet down the hill, separated by a creek that was fond of ignoring its boundaries when we got a good ole' frog-strangler.

Our place included a garden where we raised everything from potatoes to corn to watermelons, along with an orchard around which I used to practice killing myself on a Honda XR 75 dirt bike. I did my share of work such as digging potatoes the third week of June, and mowing, but mostly I was shielded from anything too hard that might retard my ability to think and go on to college so as to have a better life than my grandparents or parents had enjoyed. We were not poor, mind you, but I was loved—and part of parental love is wanting more for your children than you had.

I was the Golden Child. Smart, funny, a pretty good baseball player, the proverbial All-American Kid. I was of the generation where I was told I could go and do anything, the main purpose of my life being to "get out of here."

But on this night, all the dreams that had been dreamed for me went away, and an entirely different thing was placed in their place. Survival.

I was trapped. I could move my left hand with the "Freddie Krueger finger," but that was about it. My dear friend Michelle and another friend, Tracy, were first on the scene, driving up to what had to be an unbelievable sight—blood spattered everywhere, the smells of leaking gasoline and battery acid filling the air.

I remember coming to and not feeling normal, but not hurting yet, either. I lifted my hand up and said very calmly , "Look at my finger." It was hanging just so gingerly by that piece of skin. I was able to tilt the finger back over on itself to put the almost severed part back on top and I showed her. I have often thought of her bravery. She didn't faint, or scream, or puke in my lap. She calmly told me it was going to be OK and she was going to call for help.

I had yet to discover just how crushed my body was. The rather generous schnozz I had been born with was halfway ripped from my face. Suddenly I also had a hockey player's smile, along with various internal injuries. And my golf grip was about to require a serious adjustment now that I had my new friend Mr. Nub.

I was in that car for an hour and a half. Randy, my teammate and passenger, was freed heroically from the car by another friend who had been in charge of closing up the baseball park that night and happened upon the scene. He had a broken leg, a sprained back, and some broken teeth. (He recovered fully and went on to pitch in college for four years and become a successful girls high school basketball coach.)

Meanwhile an EMT who lived a half mile away had heard the sound of the crash. He soon arrived and began talking calmly with me. Turns out, he knew my father, who was an administrator at the local hospital. He tied a tourniquet on my leg and actually made conversation with me to keep my mind occupied until help arrived.

The rescue team arrived and worked feverishly. The first set of "jaws of life" actually broke, and they had to call for another. A wrecker was pulled in front of my car and a chain fastened to the steering wheel to lift it off my chest. Nothing like seeing a steering column being bent away from your body to get your attention.

That ninety minutes had to be the longest block of time ever for those who loved me. My parents arrived at the scene right after the rescue team, Michelle having called them. Friends who were out on the town heard and drove out. Kurt, another teammate, acted as the scout. Having to park at the roadblock, he came up to survey the damage and wisely went back and kept everyone away.

My parents talked to me, and my mother knelt beside the car as they worked. She put her purse down beside her, not realizing it was in the middle of a puddle of battery acid, which would eat holes in it later that night. It would also do a number on one of my knees. It is only now as I ride along beside my own teenage drivers that I can begin to understand what must have been racing through their minds.

When I was finally freed, all that numbness left in a blink. When they unfolded me from that car, I experienced pain I cannot begin to describe. And fear. I knew how bad it was for the first time. All the people surrounding and working knew I was in serious trouble, but I didn't—couldn't—process it.

I had never had the honor of being the focus of attention in an ambulance. In my case, I could see in the workers' faces very real concern. Their scramble to do whatever they needed to keep me stable and get me to the hospital was a disconcerting thing to watch. It was the only time that sheer panic took over me, and the only thing I remember saying as loudly as I could was, "Please don't let me die in this ambulance! Get me to the hospital first."

I knew I might be dying. So I wasn't trying to buy time to keep death at bay—I had a new and serious goal of dying in the hospital surrounded by those I loved, not in some stranger's care, valiant as it was.

Arriving at the hospital, I was quickly prepped for surgery, my hand and finger put in a bowl of ice, X-rays taken, my clothes cut off, my whole body surveyed. When I went into surgery, I felt perhaps the most peaceful I have ever felt, even to this day. Relief was coming to me, not because they would fix me, but because sleep, escape, perhaps death would find me. But the pain would stop soon.

The early damages noted: besides the newly adjusted finger, I had a crushed left ankle, a compound fracture of my right leg, a broken right ankle, and both hips were broken along with my pelvis, five ribs, and a wrist. I had severe nose damage and a missing front tooth. Other problems would make themselves known over the next month.

My friends who cleaned out my car later found my tooth, *with the entire root intact*, in the back floorboard and presented it to me. They thought that was the funniest thing they had ever seen. Nothing like good friends.

As it turns out, my missing finger is history repeating itself. Pop, my grandfather, had the same finger cut off in the same place on the *same hand*. He lost his in a much more manly way, though, cut off in a sawmill, requiring several surgeries to get it corrected properly. Mine had been cut clean as though it were a warm stick of butter.

Pop came into my hospital room and, when we were alone, told me there were things I could do with that finger that no one else could do. I asked him what, and he stuck the shortened digit up to his nostril and began contorting his face in such a way as to make one think he was picking his nose all the way to his brain.

Who would have guessed how useful that "skill" would be? I have demonstrated it many, many times since then when talking to kids—it's funny how kids love the gross stuff. Here's another useful purpose for that half digit: Years later, when I was coaching a baseball team, if a kid got hit in the head on the baseball field, I would go out to him and hold up the two fingers on my left hand. "How many fingers?" I would ask. And if the kid answered "one-and-a-half," I knew he was OK.

But back to that hospital bed and an eighteen-year-old with an eighteen year old's brain, and eighteen-year-old brains don't always fire on all cylinders. The first question I asked when I awoke from hours of surgery to save my life was, "Did they save my finger?" That was after I told the elderly nurse I awoke to that she was the most beautiful woman I had ever seen. At least I think she was elderly. I was eighteen. She might have been forty-five or something.

In about three horrible seconds, my second life began. Snatched from an All-American childhood with a loving family on Elder Mountain, I started off very alone on a path no one would choose, and my goal was about only one thing—survival. My path would prove long, and I would make it longer.

My former life had great promise. College baseball was in my immediate future. Conquering the world and making it mine would be next. Dictating, planning, willing—My Way (orchestra, please). Things would always go my way, or I made them go my way.

In hindsight, that drive was more a kind of selfishness than some great personal trait I possessed. Today some people call that determination "being driven, doing whatever it takes." Now I call it ignorance.

After waking up and proposing to Granny the Nurse, I began a journey that no one wants to take. In ICU for six days, with a total hospital stay of over a month. They had nice routines for me though—a surgery each Monday for five weeks. You think your Mondays suck! One plate, fourteen screws and roughly 47,000 surgical pins later, I was destined for a wheelchair for five months following my vacation at Hotel Hell.

For those of you who have been there, you know the drill. Humor me while I educate those who have been so fortunate to avoid a surgeon's relentless scalpel and the ensuing care that follows. When you hang out in a hospital that long, you get quite the deluxe treatment. My nighttime nurse woke me up about every seventeen seconds to take my blood pressure. What I remember is the smell of the perfume she had on. If I had to identify her in a police lineup today with Pee Wee Herman on one side and Jack Black on the other, I'm not sure I could say "That's her" in the middle—but the smell of "Eau de Strong Toilet"? Whew. I will never forget it. If I ever smell that odor again, I fear what my nightmarish sensory response might be. She must have bought it by the liter. Imported from Haiti or some other exotic outpost, I'm sure.

Whatever decent looks I might have possessed were gone. After surgery to set bones, sew up Mr. Nub and whatever else they did, I had a few touch-and-go nights in the ICU. My parents never left my side, and I cannot begin to know the level of hell they were going through. I guess I also entertained them a little, or so they tell me. I became the first person ever, who, while in traction and given morphine, pitched *and* broadcasted *every* pitch of a full nine-inning baseball game with me as a star for the Cincinnati Reds. According to my parents, that performance was followed up by me barking orders about cooking chicken at Chick-fil-A, my high school job. For some reason I never got any more morphine.

When visitors were allowed, I had an endless parade of well-wishers come through, for which I was thankful. Teenagers tend to by nature react emotionally to such a situation and travel in herds to visit and see for themselves. I realized I was in pretty rough condition, but when you go through something so shocking you don't quite grasp the enormity of it for a while. That realization was hammered home pretty quickly when a guy walked in with a few friends, took one look at me, and hit the deck. Fainted right there in front of me. Talk about a blow to your self-esteem.

At one point, I was told I had a bruised pancreas. Now I don't know what a pancreas does, but when it is bruised it hurts and makes funny stuff pile up in your belly. Of course, one of the doctors ran a test to find this out about two weeks into my stay. I had not had anything to drink by mouth during that period, so I was just a smidge *parched*. I would have killed for a glass of water. And what did the nurse do? Presented me with a twenty ounce cup and told me to drink up. When we are desperate, we forget to ask important questions. I still hate you, Mr. Liquid Chalk-giver, and I will someday hunt you down and force you to drink a drum of your elixir.

Thirsty and angry, I wasn't exactly able to get up and run. I had no choice but to lie there as "they" determined the cure for my belly bile was to jam a fire hose through my nose into my stomach. For the uninitiated, this process takes place with four large women all named Helga standing over you and holding you down while you scream for your Momma. And for Jesus to come back immediately.

The specialist assured me it was for only 24 hours. After 26 hours, I began complaining. His response was, "You can huff and puff all you want, but it will come out when I say"—which turned out to be five days of swallowing my spit while an anaconda was jammed in my gullet draining some bad stuff from my stomach. I think they bottled it for the slime used on Nickelodeon and in some Spielberg movies. Remember in *Jurassic Park* when the raptor spit that gunk all over Wayne Knight (*aka* the doomed Dennis Nedry), the guy who later played Newman on *Seinfeld*, before turning him into supper? I think that was from me.

"Dr. Huff-and-Puff's" answer got him a good shove against the wall by my father. I appreciated the gesture to be sure, and he was doing what any dad who was watching his son suffer would do.

But the truth was, I just wanted my way. It would turn out to be the first of many times to come where my way wasn't the best way.

For instance, "Nurse BM" would make her presence known shortly thereafter. Every other evening, this lovely lady would stick her head in the door and ask sweetly, "Have you had a BM today?"

Now keep in mind, at this point I had not eaten for fourteen days. I had a garden hose shoved down my throat, I was in traction from hip surgery, and I couldn't breathe well because of five broken ribs. So, I ask you, had I? That lady had a better chance of quitting her job and finding Sasquatch or the Loch Ness Monster than finding Mr. Poo in my room.

Enter the evil intern, "Thriller."

Shortly after Nurse BM's question was answered with a very weak and unknowing "no," she sent in the cleaning crew. Thriller walked in and explained the concept of the enema to me. Or maybe he didn't explain anything to me. Perhaps he told me he would still respect me in the morning. The horror of the picture that was being painted was sinking in slowly, so he could have told me I looked lovely in my vented hospital gown, for all I know. I'm not sure.

Now I am a family guy, so I will spare you the details of the fun to follow. If you need those, Google "enema"—and by all means, keep working on that GED.

"Thriller" was so named because at the first execution of his evil duties (these would be regular "play dates" for the next three weeks), he began a conversation with me that ended with his explaining he had just gotten back from seeing Michael Jackson at Neyland Stadium, where my beloved Vols from the University of Tennessee play. Can you imagine walking into a childbirth and telling someone you had just seen Larry the Cable Guy doing all his material while the husband screams "Git 'er done!" Roughly the same result ensued. Hope you had fun cleaning that souvenir shiny white glove, Thriller.

After my travels through the Horror House of Gastrointestinal Drainage, and they had finished sewing my legs back on via four more surgeries, I would get to go home. My weight had gone from a healthy and athletic 175 pounds to 117 emaciated pounds. My inability to digest food being obvious, I faced a long climb back to having a new life. I would start my new adventure a bag of bones and skin, in a wheelchair, and confined to a hospital bed set up for me at home for the next five months.

Being the loving people and good Southern Baptists they are—a belief that buttermilk biscuits are the bread of life is a requirement for membership in the SBC—my parents met the challenge head on with abundant love, and having no other way to feel like they were helping me get better, they fed me. Wonderful food. Fried eggs, bacon, and toast or biscuits for breakfast, followed by three grilled cheeses for lunch and chased down with a light dinner of steak and potatoes, and a chocolate milkshake for a nighttime snack. By the time I was finished with that wheelchair I took a good look at myself in the mirror and saw someone looking back at me whose formerly athletic body now resembled not one of my heroes like George Brett, Johnny Bench, or Thurman Munson, but had a closer resemblance to the one Chris Farley lumbered around in.

My beloved surgeon, Dr. Robert Smith, had told my parents I was going to get hungry, and for them to feed me. Now what would your mom do? What would you do for your kids?

He did not tell me to become a sumo wrestler. I began to wonder if it might be time to back away from the milkshakes when a lady tried to put one of those Japanese diapers on me and called me the "Great Butterworth-san."

Their care extended beyond just regular feedings. My Dad equipped me with a little bell to ring when I needed him in the middle of the night, and he would come and turn me, or scratch something inside one of those casts, or whatever I woke up needing. Between his eagerness to rise as often as needed and my Mother carrying out doctor's orders to feed me, I saw. . . really saw. . . what love looked like for the first time. It was never about them. They were willing to lay their life aside for mine, and instead of that being a cute phrase, they put legs on it. They did it.

But perhaps the most amazing thing to come of all this was how long it took me to recognize that love. Not just in my parents, but in the many selfless acts laid down on my behalf. You see, I thought I was the victim—I was entitled, and the world owed it to me.

Since then life has taught me one of its greatest lessons:

The world owes me nothing.

That's right. So, let me say a few things that need to be said. To the nurses, both those who took care of me and those who care today for people young and old, fat and thin, grouchy and pleasant, with the same professionalism and knowledge—you are angels and doing God's work.

Dad, thank you for the strawberry bars. Mom, I now understand as fully as I can your hurt, and the reason for all the food you nourished me with and inadvertently almost killed me with.

Thanks also to Thriller, who stopped by—thankfully without an enema—occasionally just to check on me. Dr. Garrard, my cardiologist, came in and sat down and watched golf with me one day without so much as taking my pulse. Dr. Robert Smith put me back together and did it with an astounding attitude and optimism, only to suffer a fate similar to mine when he got broken all to pieces in a car years later.

A shout-out to my sister Sandy, who gave up the summer before her senior year of high school involuntarily, but with full love, to sit with me for a month. My Pop came and sat with me each morning. Sure, he caught up on his napping, but having him snoring in my living room was somehow all I needed. Thanks, also, to my Aunt Jo. She gave freely of her time to come and feed me after Mom had gone to work.

And thanks to the note-writers. I received some of the most amazing ones, a lot of them anonymous. Folks from my mom's work even presented me with a dollar tree, which I promptly blew on chili dogs from the Burger Barn whenever my friends would stop and get me one. All of these fall under acts of kindness. Giving a little bitty bit of themselves (or in a few cases, a large chunk) and never asking for anything back, because I had nothing to give. When you're in need, you find out who your friends are.

On the Road to Real

What do you have to give? You may not be a teacher, or have eloquent words, money, power, or fame. But you have a few minutes, and someone is hurting. You don't have to know what to say. If all you have is to go sit in their living room and snore, do it.

Stop and think. Better yet, quit thinking about yourself. Or is that exactly what needs to happen first?

Is there someone you've heard about recently who has had a rough time of one kind or another? Write a name or two down here.

_____

_____

Think about something you can do to give a lift to that person. It may be big or it may be small, or it may be something in between. We're not just talking about "throwing money" at the problem, or "throwing the ideas against the wall to see what sticks." Just one thing—a newspaper rescued from the grass and stuck in the person's front door, a handwritten note, an invitation to grab a burger, a phone call or e-mail to say, "I may not have the perfect words, but I am here." Write down what you can do here—and then do it.

_____

_____

CHAPTER 2

THE TWILIGHT ZONE AND HAWAII FIVE-O

He who walks with the wise grows wise, but a companion of fools suffers harm.

—Proverbs 13:20

"I'm in a mood to do me some sinnin'."
—A Man Who Shall Be Known as "Anonymous"

I can resist anything but temptation.

—Oscar Wilde

WHAT FOLLOWED ALL that love? A happy, recovered, healthy life would have to wait. I needed to give all that pain some medicine.

After recovering at home for a year, I headed off to college at the great University of Tennessee. I wish I could tell you of four years of intense study, living life with a sense of thankfulness after my brush with death. That story would be a lie.

I have put down the following memories not out of a sense of pride, but not out of a sense of shame, either. I know people who look back on good chunks of their life with regret. If I had a do-over, I would do some things differently, as anyone who has had a conscious thought would.

Where I leave the normal thought process behind is that those times we spend wallowing in regret, for every experience we have had, the times when our heart has soared or been broken, when our emotions have been engaged fully, be it through mourning or a sunset in Maui that was too much for words, those little things pile up into who you are. Why regret them? If you are in deep pain, it is time for a time-out. Stop and collect. Be quiet, get still, and start thinking. But I am getting ahead of myself.

As Chris Gardner (Will Smith) said in the wonderful movie *The Pursuit of Happyness*, I call this part of my story "Getting a Lot of Stupid Out." My college time was a tale of two lives. The first life was lived by the new me. My body had morphed from that of an athletic All-American boy with self-esteem to spare to a new 260-pound body that my fraternity brothers referred to as "the dumpsite." I was hundreds of miles from home, with freedom to spare and virtually no self-identity. I didn't know enough to stop and think, and the people around me couldn't see that far into who I really was. They were just relieved that I was alive and in happy disbelief that I had gone from an ICU bed and multiple surgeries to a major university in just over a year.

None of us knew at that point to ask what was really going on inside me, or for healing of the deepest places of my soul, a soul that was screaming out for answers. Heck, I didn't fully realize what was happening myself at the time. Instead, the first months at UT were a time of numbness.

Like many who go away for school, newfound freedom comes with no owner's manual. Like many, I abused that freedom. The point here is the incredible need I had for getting away, running from the fact that who I was—my identity—had been destroyed. No one around me knew who I really was, and they could have cared less.

Or did they? I was far too proud to ever share my weaknesses with anyone. I wanted to stop everyone who abused me for my physical limitations and what my body had become and tell them what I used to be. Not only does the college world not want to hear that, but the world at large stands still to hear very little, for we are a world of hurry up and go, give-it-to-me-the-bottom-line thinking, and snap judgments.

But maybe I was the one who was judging. I never gave anyone the chance, never let them inside. No one would care. Shut up, plod along, survive.

And so I drank. Used drugs. Didn't go to class. Failed miserably in everything I tried to do. I quit trying. Worse yet, I quit caring. About anything. Who was I without baseball? Who was I, a fat guy with nothing left to offer? Who could love me or care about me?

Subsequently, I surrounded myself with people just like me. You ever notice that the wrong crowd is always a place of comfort for those in pain? They are other people with their own pains and struggles, but who say, "Come on in, we accept. We don't judge. Let's all feel better together." Looking back, I'd say they were generally a decent bunch, but they just didn't know how to get unstuck and as a result they just dug their heels in deeper, creating a larger hole.

I stayed high one way or another artificially for that entire freshman year. Every night brought another opportunity, and I never turned one down. When nothing was going on for us on campus, my circle would get together, get high and watch back-to-back episodes of the old *Twilight Zone* and *Hawaii Five-O* series in various altered states.

Can you imagine that scene? Can you see in your mind what Rod Serling's eyebrows or Jack Lord's sprayed helmet head look like when you're high? While the bottom of the barrel is, well, the bottom, it was a perfect place to be for the times I was living. I was living in my own twilight zone where someone had taken me away and replaced me with someone I didn't know. I was human only in that I ate, slept, and opened my eyes. Waking up would have to wait.

One of many "how low can you go?" moments came on Valentine's Day my freshman year. No date, not wanting a date, and certainly not worthy of any girl with all her teeth, I called the local pizza joint and ordered the special . . . a heart-shaped pizza . . . and had it delivered. I ate the whole thing. Alone. Do you know how depressing that is? I doubt whoever thought of that concept had a fat, hungover, lonely guy sitting in his dorm room as the company's target market. That was one crappy pizza.

Now let me ask you a question. What if? What if people had gotten to know me? Not just guzzling beer with me at frat parties, but really gotten to know me. I thought it was their fault, not caring, living their own lives. I placed the blame on them. What if I shared my heart with them, my pain? What if I had struck up real relationships where someone could encourage me? Sure, some would have walked away and had more reason for walking right past me, but we don't want those people in our lives, anyway. I am sure I passed up people who would have been lifelong friends. I will never know.

Slowly, I began to see. My grades were well past pathetic, I was a lump of human flesh, and I had no feeling.

Then I met Vicki.

Romance ensued, but to be sure, something much larger was happening. Having been through her own battles, she drew lines in the sand, began the process of showing me where life was, and more, where it was not. Perhaps most importantly, she challenged me, made me make choices.

My sense of humor returned—well, at least *I* thought I was funny. From my sixth-floor apartment on campus, I discovered a substitute for Hawaii Five-O reruns. There was a driveway directly below us! People often walked along that drive going back and forth between class, and the occasional car gave us ample opportunity for target practice. We threw everything that wouldn't hurt someone. Eggs, cheese, bologna. That last delicious treat became the weapon of choice.

Have you ever witnessed a fat guy throwing bologna out a sixth-floor window with a crowd watching along the hallway as he pegs slices of cheese on windshields or makes a Frisbee out of bologna to try and hit the top of someone's head? I assure you, there are lots of free ways to have fun, but lobbing flying bologna and cheese is an activity worthy of my own personal Moron's Hall of Fame.

Alas, it all came to an end one day. (Can you believe a former professional bologna chunker just used the word "alas" in a sentence, in context?). Some ninny, thinking he had the right to walk in class without a slice of Oscar Meyer's finest flying at him like a scud missile, backtracked his steps one day after getting wallpapered right in the forehead, waited for the offending object to whiz downward, counted apartments, and had his man.

I was let off with a slap on the wrist with a loaf of Velveeta.

I came to that fork in the road many people come to in college, if they're there long enough. I took the fork that led to graduation. My grades got back to where they should have been, I worked hard, got married, and got my degree.

Vicki had come to my rescue once, without either of us really knowing it at the time. It would not be the last time.

We got married. I called her one day from a pay phone on the famous Hill on the University of Tennessee campus, and as snow blew, I looked into vaunted Neyland Stadium while she told me the pregnancy test was positive. I was six months from graduating, we were eight months from having a baby, I had no job prospects, and the responsibilities of adulthood swirled around me like that blowing snow. Outside that, things were really breaking "my way."

Weren't they? My sphincter muscle was getting a real workout.

Growing up would have to wait. Survival mode kicked into a gear no one had told me about.

On the Road to Real

Have you made quick judgments of people and shut them out of your life? Think about a time you may have pre-judged someone's

17

looks, motives, or actions ("Don't confuse me with the facts—my mind's made up") and written the person off. Describe it here.

_____

_____

Trying to deal alone with your own pain or issues, where have you quietly passed up engaging in relationship?

_____

_____

CHAPTER 3

THE ART OF DRIFTING

The taste of defeat has a richness of experience all its own.
—Bill Bradley, basketball player,
Rhodes Scholar, and former U. S. Senator

I think everyone should experience defeat at least once during their career. You learn a lot from it.
—Lou Holtz, football coach

Experience: that most brutal of teachers. But you learn, my God do you learn.
—C. S. Lewis (Anthony Hopkins)
in the film *Shadowlands* (1993)

THERE EXISTS A real problem with surviving. We forget to live.

Now that doesn't mean we don't have fun, laugh, enjoy ourselves some, and feel alive from time to time.

I am talking about a slow drift. It can start innocently enough while we are trying to make our way. We take jobs, raise families, pay bills, and are diligent in discharging our duties.

Adulthood begins to take hold, and with it, something begins to happen. Slowly. Life begins leaking away from us one drop at a time, and we forget that we can take control of many aspects of our lives.

Days turn to months, then to years, and before we know to start asking questions, we find ourselves in a bit of a trap.

My story is no different from that of many others, and one must understand that at the point of decision about the direction your life will take is where your story will go to be born, or to die. Perhaps you find yourself here, at the great fork in the road. Slink away and exist, settling, receding quietly to the background.

Or, *show up big.*

In the movie *The Legend of Bagger Vance*, Will Smith plays the elusive, mystical caddie "Bagger" to Matt Damon's character, Rannulph Junuh. A great amateur golfer, Junuh is haunted by his memories from World War I, and has returned to his home in Savannah, Georgia, a shaken shell of his past glory. An outcast of the town because of his behavior, he is asked back into the fold in an exhibition golf match between himself and the dual legends of Bobby Jones and Walter Hagen.

The night before the match, Bagger goes out on the course with Hardy Greaves, a young boy who will act as the forecaddie for Junuh. In studying one of the greens, Hardy is putting along a line to allow Bagger to see the subtle breaks on one hole. He asks Bagger whether Junuh stands a chance, and Bagger answers, "He has to find his authentic swing." Bagger explains:

> Inside each and every one of us is one true authentic swing. Something we was born with, something that is ours and ours alone. Somethin' can't be taught to you or learned., somethin' that's got to be remembered. Over time the world can rob us of that swing. It gets buried inside us under all our wouldas and couldas and shouldas. Some folks even forget what their swing was like.

Bagger Vance is talking about something far bigger than golf.

After my wreck, I totally, completely lost my authentic swing. My Twilight Zone experience was born from a place of utter lack of identity. I had no idea who in this world I was supposed to be.

Quicker than you can read this paragraph, the person I grew up believing I was evaporated away from me. The result was being so stuck I would take any gear I could find. That gear just happened to be reverse.

The most common experience I have witnessed in people who have asked me for advice is that of being stuck like I was, of not knowing how they got where they are in their lives. Maybe they feel miserable, but most people feel something far harder to grab hold of. They've forgotten their swing. And they didn't have to have a wreck to do it. There are far less obvious ways.

Our hearts were made to be free. Not to be free of pain, but to feel as though we are fulfilling the promise that we had . . . and have. In the middle of all that adultness, of "going out and killing something for dinner and dragging it home," of carving out our place the way our granddaddies carved up the carcass—we lose our way. Being lost didn't happen overnight, but we wake up one day and ask, "What happened?"

This doesn't mean a new life, a new spouse, a new career, a new car, or a new house is going to make your troubles go away, nor are any of those fixes the answer.

Your heart, just like mine, beats to be unleashed. We all feel it. But the people who find the passion their heart swells with are those who pause to ponder, discuss, and be conscious of who they are becoming . . . or have already become.

I write from personal experience with *not* doing that at first. After graduating from college, I did what we all do. I took a job, and one I thought was going to be my career. At twenty-three, I thought I had the answer to my future. While there are rare souls that do find that place before they make mistakes that are hard to undo, I am not in that class picture.

We had our daughter, Ashley, when I was twenty-three, Vicki only twenty-one, after two years of marriage. I took a job in the insurance business and started working extremely hard to build my customer base. I put my head down to survive, yes, but I wanted to "get ahead," like many of us do, as we follow our road map that we have clearly marked for our conquests of the world.

Our son Ben would follow three years later and our little family was complete. I want to be clear that those were mostly happy times, and we shared love and raised our children with passion and purpose.

Business was good, my family intact, I had a wife who loved me, and the people who mattered in my firm said I was a rising star. Life looked grand and as though it had been tied up in a neat little package for me from the outset. We were off to the races.

I was happy. Let me make that clear: I was happy. Those were great days—but so much easy success in a person's early adult years can lead to getting off course when there is no apparent reason to do so. We may seem to have all the talent, people, and reasons to succeed. But maybe we have our head down against the wind, forging forward, carving out our place, and we forget to look up from time to time and ask the important questions:

- Am I alive in what I do?
- Am I being authentic and true to myself?

Mostly, we just get so busy we not only fool the people around us—we fool ourselves.

In my case, *life* began to happen. The career path I had laid out for myself—my way (I hear that orchestra again) began to turn in the wrong direction, taking a lot of our early hopes and dreams with it. Our finances were in a shambles, with bankruptcy in our immediate future, the result of my placing too many bets on the growth of my business and not being awake enough to entertain the possibility that those had turned into bad bets. Just not thinking, but plugging along blindly as though there were no other options. I hung on far after the passion had drained from me. Eleven years felt like they were down the toilet in lost time and hopes.

Along with a feeling of hopelessness and loss came my old friend, Pain. And I don't like Pain. I had had enough of it at eighteen to last me a lifetime. But this was a different kind of pain, and it had some things to teach me, though I didn't know it at the time.

On the Road to Real

Think about what Bagger Vance meant when he said, "Inside each and every one of us is one true authentic swing." In your case, do you have an idea of what that authentic swing—your heart, your dream, the thing that makes your heart soar—might be? If so, describe it, and if not, write down one thing you can do to discover it.

_____

_____

What do you think it means to say "Our hearts were made to be free . . .but not to be free of pain?"

_____

_____

Has "life" ever gotten in the way of your plans for yourself? Describe that time if you've had one.

_____

_____

_____

CHAPTER 4

LESSONS FROM BASEBALL PARKS AND A TEENAGER

When I was a boy of fourteen, my father was so ignorant I could hardly stand to have the old man around. But when I got to be twenty-one, I was astonished by how much he'd learned in seven years.

—attributed to Mark Twain

THOSE YEARS WERE a difficult period in our lives, make no mistake about it. It took us five years to dig out of the hole. I didn't handle the difficulties well, and my personal behavior was, to make an understatement, less than that of a model husband. But with time, I have been able to see one of the truths of our lives: As painful as my leaving my firm and having to start almost completely over was, it shaped me into who I am today. Experience was the great teacher. It taught me that when you just make decisions on the fly and don't pause to ask the important questions—the questions that I'll be asking you soon—you have no idea where you're going, and you'll get nowhere in a hurry.

In fact, it led to my lifelong desire to go into wealth management full-time. The first eleven years of my professional life were gone, but I had been prepared for a new adventure by the two things we must have to walk into these new challenges—time and experience. I was ready. In the next seven years, I climbed into the top echelon of my firm, accumulating millions of dollars and many clients under my watch-care.

Adding to that new satisfaction in my career, raising my children has been one of the great joys of my life, along with one of the great challenges. As they grew up we were at every event imaginable—dance and music recitals for my daughter, every sporting event my son has played in—over the years.

We have grown to be a very close family in spite of being attacked over the last seven years by the wickedest enemy ever created, an evil being called "the Teenager." We've even had more than one of those creatures in our house at the same time. These creatures parrot back to us in words and actions all the things we have taught them, both good and bad. We get to see the fruits of our labors and to wonder where in the world we could have gone wrong. Selfishness shows its ugly face—and sorry to admit, not just in those younger reflections of ourselves but in the older version, too, that we see every day staring back at us in the mirror as we brush our teeth—and the battle of the hormones rages right in front of us. A Teenager is an awesome force and one not to be taken lightly.

In spite of these challenges, my wife and I decided to finish the marathon we had started to turn our kids, who eventually turned into the Teenagers, out into the world as healthy, open, real, and fun people.

The force of nature that a Teenager represents can be dealt with one of two ways, and I have found how we decide to react to it is a mirror of the way we have chosen to deal with a lot of challenges we have faced or will face. Some parents flee to the hills and disappear—perhaps not physically, but they just decide to check out, armed fully with the knowledge that to stay in there, to keep battling, is so, so difficult. It is hard work.

Others decide to pick up their swords and get in the battle, and that's what we did. Vicki and I have failed to finish many things in our lives, but we made the conscious decision from the beginning to stay deeply involved with our children, knowing this was the hard course—to deal with problems as they come up, not to sweep them under the rug, but to talk openly about all the challenges we and they face and will face.

We've made many mistakes, and I am sure we will go the distance and wish we had done some things differently, but as we release our kids to the world, they will be confident in one thing: they were loved deeply by the people who raised them.

We have engaged in a lot of different activities together to forge the relationships we hope will bring a lifetime of returns. This has led to many, many hours of open discussion (at times, much to the horror of the Teenagers), trips to see things new to all of us, and various other adventures—including a recent one to install our daughter in Pigeon Forge, Tennessee, for a summer staff position with a missions organization and a full-time job at Dollywood. (Maybe the Teenager also has some good qualities . . .hmmm.)

Our son and I also took one of those odysseys during a time that seems not so long ago. When he was twelve, his baseball team on which I served as coach traveled to Cooperstown, New York for the final "hurrah" for that wonderful age in their lives. The people who created the tournament in which our team participated thought it would be a great idea if all the boys involved would stay in the barracks located on the site along with their coaches, while the parents stayed in hotels, rented houses, and other luxurious outposts. We, along with eighty-three other teams from all around the country, settled in for one very eventful week.

If you have never bunked with eleven twelve-year-olds, let me let you in on a few secrets. This is something to be experienced and never spoken of again. The smells, sounds, and thoughts of my group still haunt me. My therapy bills continue to mount.

One morning after a lovely two-hour nap where I slept with one eye open while looking for a whoopee cushion to explode in front of my face, I was sitting outside our 300 square feet of non-air-conditioned heaven looking over the fields when my son awoke and came outside. We talked about the tournament, who we were playing that day, and how great an experience it all was. And then our conversation turned to "where should we go from here."

We hatched a plan. Being lovers of baseball, we decided that since this trip marked an end to one phase of our baseball lives, we needed another project. And so our goal was born: to see all thirty major league baseball parks together before he graduated from high school.

Now, stop and think about this. Get out a map. Toronto, Seattle, Miami . . . this was not a tidy project to tackle. It would require some work and serious planning. It would require us to *drive* in Los Angeles, which should have been enough to scrap the whole idea. And I gave no thought at the time to the fact I would be doing this with a *Teenager* in tow as my travel companion.

But it fit beautifully into the goal of always having bonds with our children, and baseball was certainly a bond that we shared. I tackled the planning with my typical vigor the following winter and hatched our first trip. Chicago for two games, Milwaukee, Lakewood, New Jersey (to see a friend play minor league ball) , Philadelphia, Baltimore, and close with Philly. Five parks, seven games in five days. It was delicious insanity.

We had the time of our lives . . . in ways that we didn't expect when we started. From getting lost in a very bad part of Chicago at 1:00 A.M. (where we both found out that, yes, there are Chinese gangsters. . . . Who knew?) to getting lost in New Jersey, where, because the Teenager was threatening to die if I didn't feed him, we found perhaps the best drive-up cheeseburger and shake in the entire world, to catching a day game in Baltimore and a night game in Philly. Then there was the "memorable" experience of the Teenager having to create a men's room out of a plastic bottle in the back seat of a rented Hyundai moving in a traffic logjam at 15 miles per hour. Yup, we had ourselves a lot of pure fun.

The world had stopped. I was with my son, my beloved son, and we were on an adventure. What was I so torn up about back at the office anyway? All the financial geniuses on television would have to wait to scream at me another day. I was too busy living.

Armed with memories and eager to go again, I planned an even more ambitious outing for the next summer. On the travel agenda (I wish I were making this up) were, in order, San Diego,

Los Angeles, San Diego again, Oakland (twice), San Francisco, Anaheim and Denver. Eight games, six parks, and eight games in *six* nights, during which we took five flights. Now something very important happened during this trip.

I realized I had lost my mind.

Have you ever been somewhere that was a good time any way you look at it—a concert, a ballgame, one of your children's recitals, a baseball game where little ones are playing, really *playing*—and been unable to enjoy yourself, even had the thought inside your head that you should be having a ball but something in you holds you back?

The journey, the process of going and seeing all those parks had taken a back seat to our busyness. Have you felt that?

That great fog that clouds the mind, that whirr of machinery that goes and goes unchecked inside our heads, is the stuff that cancer of the soul is made of. I have had my share of such experiences, where I was there but I was not present. No one was home. I might as well have been watching some Discovery Channel presentation on how bugs' eyes blow in and out when they eat other bugs or some such nonsense. Wouldn't have mattered. And all the while being surrounded by the stuff I said I wanted. Friends, my family, doing things I dreamed of doing.

We had a great time, to be sure, and did we ever see some funny stuff. We still have little inside jokes that only he and I can understand, but somewhere in all that haze of activity, we lost our way. It was only after the trip was over and we were numb from exhaustion that we realized an important truth:

The goal of seeing all those parks had become our end.

Having fun, being together, sharing, allowing me to roll around in the pleasure of being with my little boy who was becoming a young man had taken a back seat to the goal.

And I realized I was living my life that way.

I had lost my authentic swing.

I began to see some lessons in the fog and to apply them to my life. The next year, we slowed down and enjoyed where we were and what we were doing. Along the way, we got to enjoy each other.

Going to New York and Boston with a stop in Hartford, Connecticut to see our friend play minor league ball again, I remembered why we were there.

Funny, when I wasn't consumed with what time the next flight was, I remembered that the time I was spending with my son would never come my way again. That sitting in Yankee Stadium just weeks before they began tearing it down was special. And that my son will never forget it, even after I am gone.

And isn't that what we are after?

Parallels with my life began to surface.

My career, always a passion until then, had become a chore. Sunday nights were especially painful, full of dread, haunted by the feeling like I had more to do with my life. The things I loved to do, my friends, my hobbies, my loves, all took a back seat to my chase, my activity. We were living at such blinding speed that time for fun, for thought, and for just enjoying those we love had gotten left on an exit somewhere along the way. I was a whirl of activity, and I had gotten lost.

As my wife and I talked one night, we tried to figure out what was missing. From all appearances, we should have been happier than pigs in mud, but instead we were looking at each other more than a little . . . tired. We had been in the whirlwind of achieving, of being the perfect parents, but mostly just . . . going . . . hard. Going where? That was our question that night. Why? What were we really up to? What were we trying to build? Was it what we even really wanted? It sure didn't seem to be leading to a life of fulfillment.

That night I began to make a rather large discovery. You either choose the hard work or it chooses you.

And then the question came. What is it that you want?

In the next chapter, I'll go into my journey toward answering that question. Is it one you have asked yourself? The questions below are preliminary ones. They'll help you find your way toward—to borrow from Regis Philbin, but I'm not being facetious in any way—The Final Answer.

On the Road to Real

Do you find yourself in a fog of busyness? Do those wheels keep turning, but with no direction that you can identify?

_____

Make a list of the things that occupy your time and your life.

_____

_____

_____

_____

Do those things line up with your life's purpose? _____

What step or steps can you take—now—to change the activities that don't?

_____

_____

CHAPTER 5

WHAT IS IT THAT
YOU WANT?

I am not interested in money. I just want to be wonderful.
>—Marilyn Monroe

If you are distressed by anything external, the pain is not due to the thing itself, but to your estimate of it; and this you have the power to revoke at any moment.
>—Emperor Marcus Aurelius, 161–180 A.D.

MY EXPERIENCE IS not your experience. But as I have progressed into my journey to being true and have observed and taught many other people, one common thread I have discovered runs through most people's lives.

I have learned that if I am feeling a certain way, I am not alone. There are others with the same worries, secret thoughts, and personal battles, and we all need permission to bring these forth and out of the dark corners of our soul.

I was awakened with a realization one of those nights. You know, the nights where you sit and mindlessly watch television, finally dozing off with the screen flashing in front of you. I was miserable. Everything felt terrible. Others had it worse, to be sure, but I had suffered the toughest year of my life, including the year of my accident.

It was the year 2008. We had buried my Pop, which I will tell you more about later. He had lived to the age of ninety and had had a wonderful, solid, happy life. I discovered something about losing a true loved one. It doesn't matter how you can justify death . . . you know the old "he lived ninety years!" spiel. It did not help my aching heart or those of my family.

When I got back to the office after the funeral, heavy-hearted and with my family on my mind, the Great Stock Market Meltdown of 2008 was underway. The business I had built was changing. Heck, the world was changing, in ways I had not seen in my lifetime. About the same time I lost a key staff member, and my career went from one of climbing the ladder of success to constantly, repeatedly having to have the same conversations over and over that involved one common theme: pain.

Pay attention. Pain again. Have you ever noticed we never stop being like little children (or the Teenager), in that we rarely learn things when everything is breaking our way? I faced the fact somewhere along the way that I needed to really pay attention and absorb the lessons being taught in every area, if only I would listen.

And that is when I realized I had not been paying attention. OK, I already had my radar up with my children, as I always had. I was aware of my relationship with my wife and that empty nest syndrome that was in the process of becoming ours. That had hit home with my daughter's moving out for college and my son getting his driver's license.

However, I had been paying so much attention to fighting the battles of my career that every other sense in my body, mind, and soul had shut down along the way. I had the sensitivity of a cactus. I had pushed friends and family away, not in so much a conscious way, but in a far more insidious way, by neglecting them. I was a poor son. I had done little to repay my parents' unconditional love—I wasn't even in regular contact with them because I was too busy, too drained, to do it. After work, I would come home, eat, and collapse into my chair, just wanting the world to shut up.

I know you will find this profound, but relationships are not built that way.

I was middle aged, discovering that parenting teenagers was really tough, and trying to walk on a couple of legs that were becoming increasingly creaky, to put it kindly. True joy seemed to have escaped me. This realization led to a question: What had I *really* done with my life?

And so the bigger question came: What do you really want?

My first gut answer, in an admittedly dead state, was . . . "money." With my moral compass still guiding me, though, I knew immediately that answer was shallow and not the real answer, or answers.

Now I would be doing you a disservice if I told you the real answers came immediately. When we are in pain, the lessons come at us hard, but only if we listen. I knew the first thing I would have to fire back up in order to answer it would be my heart.

Somewhere along the way, we all lose our heart. Business failure, broken relationships, bills and obligations, and expectations drown and overwhelm us. Things that time does to all of us. We cope by getting up in the morning, showing up at whatever we do, and surviving, hoping for something better but generally doing nothing about it. We just don't know how to get started. We lose the ability to *feel*.

Now there is more than one definition of *heart*. Besides the one from tenth grade biology—"a hollow muscular organ that by its rhythmic contraction acts as a force pump maintaining the circulation of the blood"—not that I was paying attention in tenth grade biology—you might think of words like "courage" or "character" or "affection." Here's the definition I mean: your center, the most essential part of you. That's what we've lost, and along with it, our courage, our character, even our affections, have taken a beating.

Thus the answers we chase, the gods we set up on a pedestal and find ourselves bowing to, are defective, false gods. Reflection is in order. You cannot answer what it is that you want without knowing what path you are actually on. Without knowing where we really are, we have no hope or future. Just more of the same, which is. . . not enough.

What I discovered is that I was really only about one thing. That one thing was my own comfort. Plenty of money. A healthy, loving family. A world where I didn't *have* to do much. Aside from my immediate family, I wasn't concerned all that much with other people. I just wanted me—Steve—to be comfortable. Or stop hurting. Anything. I wanted to be free. As much as anything, relief from all the short-term pressures I faced. Relief from unreasonable expectations placed on me by. . . me.

Do you know Clark Griswold? In the film *National Lampoon's Vacation*, he's the father played by Chevy Chase who is always trying to make everything perfect. He's hapless and hilarious in the movie, but in reality, that mentality is the one that gets us tied in knots. We never quite relax. We never just *be*. We're always working, grinding, striving for something. When my family started calling me "Clark," I knew it might be time to relax juuuust a little.

Freedom. That was really the answer, and I am convinced it is the answer for every man, woman or child ever born to this world. We want freedom—from the tyranny of technology, from being constantly tethered to a cell phone or a television, from noise, from obligation, from the pressure weighing on us of all the things we *have* to do, with no time left for the things we *want* to do.

I am talking about the things we *really* want, and more importantly, we need—not that new house, that big anniversary trip, not the keys to that new Prius or Porsche we've been wanting.

We really want the freedom we had when we were one of those Teenagers, those endless grocery destroyers, those younger images of ourselves who stand before us continually with hands out for the car keys or their allowance, those beings who demonstrate amazing finger dexterity (without even a glance at the keys) as they text their BFFs that message that just can't wait. BTW—this description reminds me of an incident on one of our baseball trips while Ben the Teenager and I were watching the Padres play. A lady sitting behind us leaned over and said to me, "I have been watching your son text and I have to tell you, that is the most amazing thing

I have ever seen." I said to my son, "I'm so proud." With such a skill, how can he not be a success in life?!

Maybe you have a Teenager, too, so you'll identify with what I'm saying—but if you don't know what I mean, spend some time watching them. I am more than happy to lend you mine if you cannot find any! Look for them in packs at malls, movie theaters, church, or some other place where they are inconveniently placed to shatter your peace and quiet.

They have a real talent for getting on your nerves, and you know why? *They are what you were.* Carefree and too stupid to know what they don't know and all the things and people that can hurt them. Sure, that time of life has its own challenges and it is not easy, to be sure. But Teenagers love freely, laugh easily, and just plain have a lot more fun than you do. And it irritates you, and you want to become the bitter old person that just tells them to shut up and go away, because you are too busy creating your own piece of comfort in an uncomfortable world.

As I will say several times, this whole question requires some meaningful thought. Otherwise, you might end up like my daughter. Coming in from her part-time job one night, she said, "Dad, tonight while I was at work I came up with a theory. Why do we have money? We don't need money. If everyone just gave everyone else what they needed, we wouldn't have to have money. It would solve a lot of problems in the world."

I began explaining the concept of incentive to her, that people would not get up and go make cars, or televisions, or drugs that cure disease without incentive. Seemingly not fazed, she told me, "Well, I am going to develop my theory, and I am going to make a lot of money off of it!" This is the same daughter who was with us as we returned a rental car to the airport. A police car on patrol in the parking garage passed as we drove to the rental booth, and she said, "Wow, Daddy, that man rented a police car. I didn't know you could do that."

I will let the irony rain on you while I say, yup, these are my children. Thank you. Thank you very much. Really.

What, or who, robbed us? And how did it happen? I am betting the culprit lies right between your ears.

Expectations. We expect perfection from ourselves. How many of us have thought, "My life has not turned out the way I hoped." Primarily because we expected perfection. The perfect spouse, kids, home, career, and with those established, then would come money, things, status, power, reputation—all the spoils.

And it cannot happen. The world you dreamed of is not possible. Your spouse cannot be perfect any more than you can. Your kids are guaranteed to break your heart because they are *just like you*. The air conditioner will go out in your house. Cars will break down. Careers get sidetracked, layoffs happen, people mistreat other people.

We also suffer from the expectations of other people, some of whom have your best interest at heart, but who mostly have their own agenda—namely, how you can contribute to their own status, reputation, power at work, or profiting from you in general.

We have to be the exemplary spouse, the perfect parent, and plenty of information screams at us how to do it! Get busy, because you aren't good enough.

Look: improving yourself is a good thing, and a process that takes some time. And it is needed for you to fulfill and use the talents and gifts you have been given. But there is a vast difference between working on ourselves and walking around in constant guilt that we are not good enough, that our dreams and expectations are not being met because we don't have what it takes.

Here is the meat of the problem. We walk around feeling all these things in very deep, secret places, and as life piles up around us, we bury them deeper to take care of the task at hand.

And so we live in quiet agony. All these dirty little secrets imprison us, the thoughts we don't want anyone to know. We hide from everyone our true feelings, what is really going on in those little corners of our soul we don't take the time to clean because we fear. When we feel like we are just getting too full of all of those bottled feelings, we don't dare tell anyone what is really,

really going on because we are scared of what people might really think of us.

We're scared we might lose all that stuff we create, telling ourselves that it's what we're supposed to be and have. Will they still love me? What will happen to our reputation? Will they think I am crazy? Am I crazy? Why don't I just shut up, toughen up, suck it up, and move on?

Because that stuff is killing you, robbing you of your joy, your fun, your purpose. Without expression and with fear, we are doomed to get to the end of our life and wish we had lived a little more dangerously, loved a little freer, laughed a lot more, chased our dreams and damn the consequences, and not been as tired, as bitter, and accepting the status quo as "just the way it is."

I say no! I reject that I cannot dream, love, laugh, live uncomfortably, and learn to know that the struggle itself is sweet, to understand that the lessons are buried and earned through that very struggle. But the struggle is the process. It doesn't have to *be* a struggle.

We cry for freedom. Sweet freedom. Men and women have died to protect yours. Why are you dying in that prison of the soul?

And how long will you allow yourself to be a slave?

Most people walk around knowing, absolutely knowing— falsely—that they are not *enough*, that they do not have what it takes. That the very minute someone gets to know the real me, they won't like me anymore, that I will end up alone, that the world will laugh at me.

A wonderful illustration of this was one of the final scenes of the movie *Good Will Hunting,* where Matt Damon is Will, a closet mathematical savant, who works as the janitor of a school where he anonymously shows off his skills by solving mathematical equations on the blackboard during the night shift. Robin Williams, a professor in the film, is also the therapist who tries to let Will's genius out for the world to see and benefit from.

Throughout the film, Will does a great job of sabotaging himself and short-circuiting any aid that comes his way. Haunted by a terrible past, he is unable to share the great burdens that lie within and hold him back. The therapist, with storm clouds of his own in his rear view mirror, has gotten close but has been unable to crack Will's shell. In that telling scene, a session begins with the therapist saying, "It's not your fault."

Will rebuffs the depth of the comment with a shallow "I know." The scene is comprised of the therapist repeating over and over the same, powerful, core-splitting words, "It's not your fault." With each repetition Will breaks a little more, before retreating behind a shroud of vulgar, angry words meant to fend off the challenge to his posing. When the therapist's words have to be considered over and over, the emotions of a lifetime of self-doubt, self-hatred, shame, and fear finally come pouring out of Will. Seeing that happen is hard to watch.

But the same thing needs to happen in many of us.

It's not your fault. The striving, the rushing. Presenting the perfect face to your church, your classmates, your colleagues. Showing everyone how successful you are. How powerful. How much money you are making. No cracks in your armor. No, sir. Showing folks no fear, no weakness, and in some cases telling them by your actions to be just like you.

It's not your fault. In an annual planning meeting once of a group of people who ran their own small businesses, I heard a man say, "My goal for this year is not to try so hard." A stroke of genius. This statement came from a man who had lived through all that earnest trying, the grand straining effort to get it all right, but had discovered that no matter how much effort he gave it, how many hours he spent, it wasn't enough. He didn't measure up to the standards he had for himself.

It's not your fault. Stop doing so much and focus on who you are. As my friend has often told me in counsel, be, and then do. Focus on who you are, and the *do* part of who you are becomes a natural outpouring from that center.

You will never be enough to overcome the shortcomings that you have decided you have. The things that were pounded into your head by bullies, friends who stabbed you in the back, jealous enemies. Misguided parents. But worst, your faults are highlighted in your own brain from the observation of all the other perfect people in the world. All the folks you have watched who just seem to have it all together. "Why can't I be more like them?"

The things we believe about ourselves that are untrue are astounding. A shockingly low number of people really know themselves. We are too busy. We don't know who our neighbors are, let alone what is happening and being spoken into our very own souls.

Why don't you ask *the* question: What do I want? What do I really want? Compare what it is you *say* you want and line it up with how you are living your life. What you say vs. what you do: When these goals don't match up, they hinder us. Fear takes over, and we need to identify it and run into that fear at all costs.

David vs. Goliath. The fascinating thing about this story for me is not that David won, although if it happened today it would make every Top 10 List, and ESPN would show the televised pay-per-view highlights on a continuous loop about seven thousand times. The amazing thing is that when told to enter the fray, David didn't just step into the ring. He took off the equipment his father had given him, found five stones, and grabbed his slingshot. He stuck with what he knew. He didn't try to be someone he wasn't. Next, we are told he did the most amazing thing. As the person everyone most feared moved closer, David *ran quickly toward* the battle line to meet him. He didn't walk, he did not tiptoe. He ran at his fear.

When is the last time you ran at your fear? It must be defeated. Fear of the unknown. Fear of being known. Being afraid of those things that, yes, could happen, but what are you doing worrying about those anyway? What are you going to do about them? You control none of the "coulds" or "maybes" with worry.

And what is that fear getting you, anyway? Ever lay awake at night staring at the ceiling playing the "what if" game? You know, where you take every piece of your life and dissect it and come up with every possible thing that could go wrong with it? And then envision it happening. Go ahead, pick someone and talk about the things that scare you the most. Life will not happen to those sitting around and waiting—we have to go and meet it. Run quickly towards it.

Cowering at the fear of being fully known, being afraid of living a real, transparent life—it's a lie to think you can be happy if you hide the real you from yourself and others. Walking on eggshells, failing to deal with problems and only seeing them compound as they go unaddressed. . . .How is that working out for you?

The second thing within us that we must fight against is the fact that we will avoid pain at all costs. Having more experience at this than I would choose, I can tell you what perhaps you already know. Pain is the great teacher if we will allow it. If we can set aside our selfishness to know what it is that we are to learn.

Now most sane persons would not deliberately seek out pain. And I am sane at times, so I will tell you running from pain is the proper and natural response—most of the time. However, there are reasons not to be afraid to allow pain into your life.

If you start asking *the* question, you are going to get answers, but not before a long look in the mirror begins to instruct you. Press the pause button on all the noise. Look, and you'll begin to see that most people, yourself included, are not living the life they imagined. Stuff got in the way. You can fill in your own blanks, as you have your own unique story. Just stop. And ask.

Why? Why have you let life happen? To seep in, in its insidious ways. And you look up and don't like what has accumulated?

One of the occupational hazards of living a life of truth telling is that it will attract people to you—kind of like all the pins and screws in my "bionic" legs attract the notice of the electronic metal detector in the airport security line. I have had the opportunity to sit with several couples whose relationship was in distress. Relationships run into trouble for an endless number of reasons, but it boils down to one thing. We don't talk to one another in meaningful and truthful ways, even the ones we are supposed to love the most. Pain being the primary hurdle, we don't want to let anyone, even the one who loves us the most, inside us to know what goes on in our private moments.

The couples I know who have survived such painful episodes are stronger than they have ever been, but it did not come without a price. Pain, tears, having to admit our weaknesses and to lay our defensiveness aside are not a whole lot of fun. But what is your alternative? Perhaps even worse pain, as we deal with the fallout of a broken marriage or relationship and we *don't* deal with the things inside us that caused us to get in that spot in the first place, dooming ourselves to repeat our mistakes if we continue down the road we're on.

The pain that will come is perhaps the healthiest thing you could ever hope for. That small, almost silent sound you will hear will be your heart. And it will be saying "thank you." For after the time you have spent piling up walls around your heart just to get by, climb the ladder, raise kids, chase what you thought were the right things but only to find them strangely hollow, it will begin a release that will bring you—well, alive. Maybe for the first time in years.

This pain I invite you to is a giver of life. Are you spending your time around people who feed your soul with good things? Do they offer you nutrition for your spirit? Or have you done like I did in my own little twilight zone and surrounded yourself with people you *might* like, but who have no interest in asking the hard questions and coming out of the rut?

On a phone call one day with a client, the subject of keeping an inheritance intact or not waiting to give it to her adult children now came up. She told me she and her husband had decided not to give the money right now, even though the children currently had financial needs. Before you race to judgment, hear her next words. "My husband and I thought about it and determined that 'the struggle is sweet.' The places where we learned and where we became closest were in the tough places. And I don't want to rob them of those experiences."

Now there was a time when I would not have understood that. Give them the money, help absolve the stress, the pain. Make things easier. But her words resonated deeply. We *know* this is where we learn, yet we do everything we can to avoid those circumstances.

Heed these words. Pay attention in your struggle. Hear. Listen. Lessons are being taught.

Stop and think. Are you giving yourself to things that give you energy? Or are all your hours spent in things and people that do nothing but take from you? I have some really tough news for you. All those things you think could not go on without you? They will.

You are not as important as you think. Sorry. What will happen? As you find your true call, your own voice expressed from deep within the heart, your purpose, you will be a giver of life even stronger than before, but it will be authentic. Operating in your purpose, you become even *more* important. That is exactly the moment when you really become indispensable.

I would invite no one to physical pain or volunteering for the emotional variety. After eight surgeries and more to come, it is not a burden I would wish on anyone else.

But get this: I wouldn't take anything for it. Oh, I dream about what might have been. How would my life have turned out? What would my baseball career have looked like? Would the twilight zone have been avoided? What would I have done for a living? What would it feel like to run again, to get out of the bed in the morning without all the popping and grinding of bones and going to the shower for the relief of hot water pouring over my limbs to wake up? To not hurt going up a flight of stairs?

To which I answer this way: What is the point? The reality of my getting creamed by that Chevelle is that it shaped my life. I went to school at the University of Tennessee, which is not where I was going to play baseball. There I experienced the twilight zone. But I also experienced the beginning of a new dawn.

I had to grow up. I would have never married Vicki, who has (sometimes foolishly, in my judgment) walked by me for twenty-one years. I would have never known Ashley and Ben. I would have been robbed of the three people I love the most in the world!

I would have never been able to talk with people going through their own pain and then listen with an ear that really does know what it is like to have one life snatched away and replaced by another one not asked for. The reasons I can fulfill part of my purpose of being available to other people are not only the physical pain I went through, but the emotional fallout I experienced. The things Vicki and I dealt with in our own marriage have given me, if I am open enough to share them, understanding of what they're also going through.

See? That pain equips me, and it can equip you. Once we are away from the rawness of our experiences, all that stuff becomes powerful. It means freedom for you and makes you someone who by your very presence and sharing of your story can have impact.

It means you can put the fear of being known aside. It means starting with those closest to you. Taking the risk of being fully known to them is in reality not a risk at all. If people close to you really love you, if they are really your friends, they'll want to know you. They'll want to get real with you, and you with them. When those who matter know you fully, there are no skeletons left in the closet. What you see is what you get. So what's there to be afraid of?

It means showing up big in someone's life.

All your past failures, tragedies, wounds, and injustices have woven together. They are who you are. No matter what they are, you find yourself where you are. Grieving over them after a time makes you . . . someone else. Someone who has lost heart.

In the New Testament book of Matthew, chapter twenty, there is a scene outside the town of Jericho where Jesus comes upon two blind men sitting by the side of the road. They must have hoped to be in his path—they've heard the word-of-mouth about how people have been healed by his touch. When they hear Jesus passing by, they shout, "Have mercy on us!"

Now note the two things that unfold next. First, the crowd tells them to be quiet. But out of a place where they desperately recognize their need, they shout all the louder, "Have mercy on us!"

Jesus stops, pauses, and responds with the question of all questions. "What do you want me to do for you?"

Now, my beliefs about who Jesus is inform me that Jesus didn't have to hear what they needed—he could have healed them even without them asking—but he wanted them to speak the desires they had. They did, and he did. For the two blind men, the need was physical. For many of us, it is something far less obvious.

What you did with all that stuff in your past makes no difference now. What you do today, what you do tonight, is all you have.

Do it. Open your heart. Write it down. Call it out. That's how this book started, and I can't shut up. You won't be able to, either— and that's a good thing.

On the Road to Real

What is it that you want? Exactly? Think about it first. Then write down what you really want.

_____

_____

Compare or contrast what you wrote to what you are doing. Do those two answers line up?

_____

What would you do if you were not afraid?

_____

What would you do if you knew you would not fail?

_____

When is the last time you shared those answers with someone?

_____

Have you ever answered these questions before now ?

_____

If you haven't, will you now? _____

CHAPTER 6

HIDING

. . . the truth will set you free.

—Jesus, in Matthew 8:32

If only I had a little humility, I would be perfect.

—Ted Turner

RIDING DOWN THE road this week with my son, I asked him one of the thousands of questions I have asked him during our times together driving around in my pickup truck. He currently doesn't have a girlfriend. I asked him what he looks for in a girl and what makes someone attractive to him.

His answer is true for everyone, but it speaks to a deeper truth. He told me, "The primary thing that attracts me to anyone is that they aren't fake, but they are a real person."

Aren't you attracted to those people? Think of those you have been close to over the years or have admired, and I will bet you will see a pretty common thread. We are attracted to genuine people—folks that love and live openly.

Yet we all have things we hide. We have little walls built in certain places. You hit that wall pretty quickly when you try to get to know some people, but with others, the wall is hidden and you don't run into it right at first. But we all hide things behind our walls that we would prefer others never knew.

Why we hide says more about what we believe about ourselves than about some hidden agenda. The why we hide reveals the what we believe about ourselves. Ultimately, maybe you believe that deep inside, you don't have what it takes. Maybe you believe that if others find out what you are really thinking about yourself, you would somehow seem smaller to them. Maybe you think if the truth comes out, everyone would know that you think you're not bigger than your challenges. You would show yourself to be a victim—which, by the way, you aren't.

You would appear weak.

I walked around inside this walled-off place for many years. My twilight zone experiences were something I walked around hiding, along with many other things that happened in my early adulthood. How could I lead people? What would my kids think if they really knew the truth? What about my parents? Most people would certainly frown on such activities.

Until I learned they were just like me.

Even later, I never wanted to appear to be "the jerk" at my business. I had a hard time sharing my feelings with staff and clients—my fears, my expectations, the fact that I didn't always roll out of bed fired up to "hunt ducks with a rake," as a friend of mine once said.

Now wait a minute. Share with people on your payroll? People who come to your church classes to, yes, be together, but also to hear something of value you have to say? Be straight in front of your clients? I cannot talk to those people that way. I have to be *on*.

Having to be *on* all the time is at the very essence of what is wrong with us. Never be wrong. Always listen but don't *hear*. The point of talking with someone one-on-one is so that you can jump in and spout off your pearls of wisdom. One-up everybody. Appear to have it all together and figured out.

Have you seen the evidence of hiding in yourself or in others? Left alone long enough, hiding behavior exhibits several marking characteristics. Folks who act a certain way have a reason for acting that way. We walk around with false pride, arrogance, and an anger that boils just below the surface. Something gnaws at us, and we can't even really put a name on it. Our frenzied pace driving us, we never pause to examine its cause.

We share an awful lot of the same battles. Sure, you probably don't have legs that creak with every move you make as mine do, legs that look like some of Dr. Frankenstein's best work, but your hurts are there. And you have many of the same questions I have had. Am I enough? Why do I feel this way? I should be fulfilled. What's wrong with me? Am I really an adult? I still feel like a kid. I didn't ask for all this stuff that's on my plate. How did I get here?

My daughter Ashley gave me a wonderful example of how we hide even in the most obvious of situations. One summer night my wife and I were sitting inside, enjoying a relatively peaceful night as Ashley and a friend pulled out of our driveway to go be with friends. My beloved pickup was parked in a place that was a little more difficult to see than normal. In her rush, she backed into my truck.

As I sat inside unknowingly talking with my wife, my daughter the Teenager exploded into the house (as is her norm and that of many of her breed, as I've been told). "Dad, I backed into your truck, and I think I broke the little Nissan emblem on the front!" she excitedly told us. The trembling in her voice betrayed her juuuust a little. I nervously got up and walked outside to see what the damage was.

Now, I know my daughter pretty well. She told me she cracked the emblem on the grill of my truck, but allow me to interpret what she meant to say. The following phrasings are what she intended.

"Dad, I backed up my car at approximately forty-five miles per hour, and not knowing you were so stupid as to park your truck where it was (after all, this is your fault), the cast iron trailer hitch on my car rammed, full-throttle, into the truck. The hitch entered your engine through the emblem area of the grille, where it then bent your radiator like an accordion so that fluids from it are gushing down the driveway. It also rearranged your engine creased your hood in half, and bent the front end so badly you cannot open your doors."

More than five thousand dollars in damages proved my interpretation to be closer to the truth.

Now, where was the victory, and what relief was there, in not immediately telling me the full truth? The truth was going to come out at that very moment. Yet her first impulse, like that of all of us, was to hide the truth and avoid the inevitable pain, even if for only a few short seconds.

Oh, that's just the reasoning of a scared Teenager, you say. Really?

My wrecked Honda and my even more wrecked body twenty-five years ago left me with many questions that have been answered and continue to be answered. Let me give you an example: One night recently I was in my son's room talking with him about things that were going on in his life. Baseball was proving to be a real struggle for a lot of reasons for the first time in his life, and he was wondering whether or not he would really miss it if he just quit.

Much to my surprise, I thought back to being in the hospital after my wreck. I was quiet for a minute, recalling exactly how I felt. And I began sharing it with him. Deep stuff. Straight from the deepest place in my heart.

I realized I had never shared my hurt in this area with anyone. It may seem obvious, but I had never said it out loud. I told him of lying in that hospital bed, and one day someone brought me the local newspaper. One of my teammates was on the front page being mobbed at the plate by my former teammates after hitting a home run against our main rival.

"That's great. I am happy for him," I said. And I was. But I was overwhelmed by an ache deep inside me. For the first time, the full weight of the game being taken away from me rained down on me. It was over. I would never, ever have those experiences again. It had been ripped away from me, and there was nothing I could do about it.

I wept in front of my son as I told him the story. I hope I made it clear to him that I want him to play for his reasons, but to be sure he is finished with something before he lays it down. There are times you don't know how much you love something until it is gone. The truth I was able to share from my own experience was that I had felt the same way shortly before my accident, for a lot of reasons. But my love for baseball was only fully evident when it had been taken away.

I am not really sure what he took from our time, for he will have to make his own decisions. But you can be sure of one thing. He got all of me, and he knows his father's heart. Isn't that all we can do for those we love?

And what had I missed out on in not earlier sharing that out loud? I had hidden my feelings out of love for my family. They had enough issues of their own to deal with, and the last thing I wanted them worrying about was any further emotional scars, as there had been plenty of physical ones to concern them. Perhaps I hadn't been ready until the perfect time and the perfect person in the perfect situation was able to hear me. One other thing. What would my son have missed had I kept that locked away? Time will tell his own decision, but I feel sure he will not forget our time together that night. If I had kept it hidden, he would have missed an important part of me.

We are good at judging the evil we see in the world. But you know what we never pay attention to? Grace. We fear the judgment of others and of God, but spend precious little time on the grace that has been shown to you and me in our lives. Grace is something given without merit. It is not what we necessarily deserve.

What have you experienced more of in your life, judgment or grace? I asked this question one day in the class I teach at church, and people were quick to say God had shown them a lot more grace than they deserve, but other people had shown more judgment than grace. Perhaps this is your experience, as well. So my follow-up question is this. What have you shown more of? Perhaps we could all stand to give out more grace than is our quick, knee-jerk nature.

Judging others says more about us than it does the person we are judging. In *My Utmost for His Highest*, Oswald Chambers wrote, "Stop having a measuring rod for other people. There is always one fact more in every man's case about which we know nothing."

What about that old judgment stick? Do you use it? How about other people using it on you? How many people, after all, know everything about you? Should they judge your actions without all the information?

In one coaching session I had with a client who was in charge of a large staff and had many, many eyes dissecting his every move, the subject of that judgment and his own priorities came up. The main reason we hide is to avoid that very judgment of others. In his case, he had a choice. He could worry and stew about what his coworkers thought of him, or he could put his family's needs first, which was what he really wanted to do. He could prioritize his responsibilities by separating out the ones that lined up with his giftedness and skills. Then he could encourage his employees to line up their own gifts, talents, and goals to the remaining duties and take ownership of those responsibilities—even if they were things people had previously expected *him* to do.

At the same time he could make his family his number one priority. If he does, he might risk people being bothered by some of his choices. If he doesn't, he can bury himself in his work, giving his life to that cause, at certain harm to himself and his family. And even if he makes that choice, people might still line up with their critiques and be displeased over something—because they always are, aren't they? In this situation, either way he invites that judgment, so why not come out of hiding and do what he really wants to do?

Your situation is no different. Don't make your choices based on what other people might think. You cannot win that battle. Don't pick it. The judgers aren't people you want to build your community with, anyway.

God's grace has abounded in my life. Looked at strictly on its merits, a good chunk of my life would indicate that what I *deserve* is not what I have gotten. My wife has shown me grace on many occasions when I have not been exactly the white knight she thought she was getting when she said, "I do." My children, parents, and friends have shown me grace when I didn't measure up, and like most folks, that has been too often.

My friend Boyd coached baseball with me through all the years of our sons' careers and was always challenging me. A "yes man" he was not. Kind of a tough guy, Boyd was a real hard case when we first met. "Fun" was not exactly his middle name when it came to baseball. Yet, for my friend Greg and me, fun had become our way of doing things. We coached hard and we taught and expected our boys to play hard, but we laughed more sitting on baseball buckets than anyone should in a lifetime.

One day in a particularly tense game in the state semifinals, we were all in our zone, and my role was to call pitches to the catcher. Now, I had a terrible habit of chewing tobacco when I coached. (And let's hold off on all the emails right now telling me how terrible that was in front of the kids. I know. Show me some grace.) This was quite the warm day, and I had just put in a big, fresh batch. Now, when you chew tobacco, you spit, and it is not clear. Boyd always sat next to me while we played defense, and he and Greg would offer advice, particularly when I didn't want any. I was turned toward the catcher giving signs when, unbeknownst to me, Boyd got up to get a drink of water. At the perfect moment, I gave the sign and turned to, ah, expectorate. If you are from the South, that means "spit." A lot. A keg-o-spit. And Boyd's timing was perfect. I covered him from his elbow down to the tip of his fingers.

Now, I don't know what in your life calls for a tail whoopin' but that probably should make the list. Boyd is a pretty strong guy, and in the middle of this intense game that our whole season had built up to, we had ourselves a situation on the side. I sat in slack-jawed amazement at what had just happened, while Greg and the kids on the bench nearly peed themselves from laughing so hard.

I braced myself, waiting for the deserved series of blows about my face and head. But as I sat waiting and looking at my soon-to-be-killer, he did the most curious thing. He started laughing. Now he had a comment or two and made sure I knew what I deserved, but he grabbed a towel, wiped it off, and chalked it up as a funny story.

Boyd's reaction wasn't what I deserved. I wonder what he'd think of me using the Tale of the Traveling Tobacco Juice as an illustration for grace. But how he behaved is an example of what grace is. It surprised us all. How many people in your life would surprise you? Given a chance, you will likely find out the people that love you will look past your faults. And love you more.

Do you see how we cram this stuff down our own throats, swallow the bitter taste, and hide all of our feelings because we are supposed to be tough? How we move on because the next thing on our to-do list beckons? How we show everyone how "fine" we are doing? How this false front erodes us piece by piece? Only to surface at the most inopportune time? You continue to do that and the bill comes due, and sometimes it's too late to pay it.

What are you hiding? The misery you feel in your work? The unhappiness you feel in certain areas of your life? The unfulfilled promise of your purpose? What hidden areas of your heart are off-limits to your spouse? A broken dream that stalks you? Or are you hiding from the elephant that is not even in the room? You know, the things that are obvious in a relationship that go unsaid. Most of us walk around being scared of the elephant that *is not even there.* Here's what I'm getting at: How many of your fears are of things that aren't even on the today-in-reality radar?

We worry about things that *might* happen. I have bad news. A lot of things *might* happen. But if you play that game long at all, I can guarantee what *will* happen.

Given time, all those things will boil over and become exposed. We get divorced, complaining, "My spouse doesn't understand me." We find our children aren't listening to us. And why should they? They don't know who and what we really are and that our advice comes from honest, authentic places. Without that transparency our words just become noise, and they have no connection with our understanding of what they are going through. Not only our families but also our friends will pull away when we put up that wall, because they cannot fully know our hearts and our truth.

A story I read once explains what I'm trying to say better than I can:

> There was a little boy visiting his grandparents on their farm. He was given a slingshot to play with out in the woods. He practiced in the woods; but he could never hit the target.
>
> Getting a little discouraged, he headed back for dinner.
>
> As he was walking back he saw Grandma's pet duck.
>
> Just out of impulse, he let the slingshot fly, hit the duck square in the head and killed it. He was shocked and grieved! In

a panic, he hid the dead duck in the wood pile, only to see his sister watching! Sally had seen it all, but she said nothing.

After lunch the next day Grandma said, "Sally, let's wash the dishes."

But Sally said, "Grandma, Johnny told me he wanted to help in the kitchen."

Then she whispered to him, "Remember the duck."

So Johnny did the dishes. Later that day, Grandpa asked if the children wanted to go fishing and Grandma said, "I'm sorry, but I need Sally to help make supper."

Sally just smiled and said, "Well, that's all right because Johnny told me he wanted to help."

She whispered again "Remember the duck." Sally went fishing and Johnny stayed to help.

After several days of Johnny doing both his chores and Sally's, he finally couldn't stand it any longer.

He went to Grandma and confessed that he had killed the duck.

Grandma knelt down, gave him a hug and said, "Sweetheart, I know. You see, I was standing at the window and I saw the whole thing. But because I love you, I forgave you. I was just wondering how long you would let Sally make a slave of you."

Hiding turns us into slaves. Dragging shackles of our own making, we walk around scared we will get found out. We just know how they will react when they discover that we don't always think the right way, that something gnaws at us, or that others are better than we are. We've thrown up a wall, and it becomes a barrier to keep out intimacy and real relationship. Why?

Again, how's that working for you?

And again, I ask: How long will you allow yourself to be a slave?

At one point as I was struggling with being truthful about all of me—my past, my fears, the things that haunted me—I spoke with my friend Gary about what laying it all out there would look like and asked him how he felt about doing it, just having the ultimate puke session. His response summed up what I suspect most of us would feel if we were honest with ourselves. He said simply, "It scares the hell out of me."

We laughed a little uneasily because his answer expressed pretty well how we both felt. For the time being, we moved on, but the need for transparency still rumbled underneath the surface for both of us. You can only bury the truth for so long once it has been brought to your conscious attention that you do, indeed, have things that are enslaving you, things that are holding you back. Not engaging willfully in truth telling is dangerous . . . and lack of honesty with yourself will eventually come and find you.

True, some people die with their secrets. Man, I don't know about you, but that makes my stomach just hurt. I reject living a life of fear. I chose to *unhide*, and I vow to never do it again, as tough as that is at times.

I am an expert in this area, and I say that with a good deal of regret. I went through a good professional part of my life playing a role, putting on the face, being *on*. Never, ever communicating my fear, my failures, with anyone, my wife included. A day of reckoning came (more on that later), but until that time I spent some years in a prison of my own ideas of what and who I was supposed to be. How was I supposed to look? How was I supposed to act?

I had a mental image of myself that I thought was "me." It combined with the expectations of other people into "the ideal Steve." That Steve drove and informed everything I did and every role I had: businessman, husband, father, successful young man.

Arrogance is the enemy. I got to see this first-hand. I was helping put together a program for a men's ministry event. We had a great desire for it not to be just an event but something real that would equip men going forward. We were working on how to provide some ongoing support after the weekend was over.

During the course of planning, we invited leaders from area ministries for a series of meetings about subject matter, classes, and the true everyday issues we had discovered were facing men in the real world. The men we had talked to struggled with issues of sex, addiction in any number of forms, anger, and feelings of failure. They felt they didn't measure up to the standard the world had set for them.

Well. . .here's what happened: In short, our belief that most men were dealing with these and other issues alone and in private, and that they were being held captive to them, was met with some resistance from these leaders. They didn't take well to our notion that they might have some of the same issues too, and in fact, might be in more danger than the people they lead precisely because of their leadership platform.

You would have thought we had burned the flag or talked bad about good biscuits—and either one of those offenses is cause for a whoopin' where I grew up. Hearing that we thought leaders themselves might be struggling like other men was insulting, I suppose. And to add injury to the insult, the uncomfortable thought that the men under their guidance were in a world of trouble was almost too much. Tension ensued, and I am afraid I did not do much to help the situation.

What hit me much later, though, was not the arrogance of some of the leaders we met with. I realized we all had some of the same arrogance. We expect—a better word might be "demand"—too much from our leaders, church or otherwise. We expect perfection, and we don't like dealing with anything less. We may be hurting, but we do not want to see weakness in the people who are supposed to have it figured out. In the South, we might say, "We'll just take them out back." Where I come from the phrase has a meaning more like "Let's go outside and settle this once and for all." In other words, we'll just judge those people, dispose of them, and move on.

Or do we? I would submit that leaders who show us their warts are more attractive. Struggling out loud leads to sympathy for the struggler from nearly everyone but the most arrogant. Now, by "struggling" I don't mean wallowing in one's misery or celebrating one's failures, but I do admire people who are honest enough to talk about the fact that they do struggle. Do you? You know where the magic in this lies?

It gives us permission to struggle right back.

It is from this acknowledgement of our struggles that bonds and community are formed. An odd thing happens when we are released from the prison of our minds. The people who love you will love you not only in spite of it; they will love you even more, and more deeply. Real relationships are built this way. Think of your closest friends. A common refrain as we describe these friendships is this: "He (or she) knows everything about me."

It is precisely because your friend knows everything about you that the bond is so real. Your biggest ally is that person who knows you best. Here's the reason why: those closest to us see ourselves better—and truer—than we see ourselves, and that is a good thing. We walk around with blind spots in our eyes about ourselves. We sometimes cannot see well because we are on the inside looking out, and we can't see ourselves as others see us.

So why are we afraid to enter these authentic relationships? Maybe because they invite pain. Sometimes the truths that friends and loved ones make you confront about yourself can hurt. But pain can be a good thing. "No pain no gain" is a proverb that isn't only true in fitness training. When you learn your own weaknesses, you grow in empathy toward others and your story can help others who are struggling.

I coached my son's travel baseball teams for ten years. I built some relationships with parents and the young men I coached that have borne good fruit. Coaching was a commitment of time, energy, and money that is hard to explain unless you have done it for yourself.

I think I was a good coach, but I made some mistakes. My glaring weakness was that I loved to argue with umpires.

I was the worst kind of coach for an umpire. I had been around the game all my life, knew the rules, and had been an umpire myself for twenty years. I knew a lot, and was not afraid to tell them what was what when they made a mistake. I could sling the insults at the umpire faster than a lounge lizard can use his pickup lines in a Holiday Inn bar on a Saturday night.

I was an expert at taking jabs at the ump through my kids, yelling such encouragement as, "Don't you *ever* swing at that pitch!" when he would call a particularly poor pitch a strike against one of my kids, or, "Throw it through the clown's mouth" when the strike zone got too tight for my taste.

I think most people saw my "enthusiasm" as entertaining, and it rarely—and thankfully—resulted in anything major. One day, though, while we were playing in a tournament in our home town, a well-respected man in our community was behind the plate as we played a heated rival of ours, and the game was tight. I yelled at one particular pitch that did not go our way, and as I crossed the plate to go back to the dugout, the man expressed his displeasure privately to me.

Later in the week, word had leaked around about my small but vocal outburst. My friends sat me down and told me the implications of what I had done, and they were deeper than a missed strike call in a baseball game.

I'll tell you what they did. They hurt my feelings. They got in my cabbage, as we say in Tennessee. I had given them permission to get in my life, and they jumped in with both feet. They had made the decision that they loved me enough to tell me the truth, unedited. There was no fight-back in me, although my first thoughts were defensive, because I knew they were right. I didn't like having someone sit me down about my faults, but a moment of truth was sorely needed.

I wrote a heartfelt apology to the opposing coach and the umpire followed up by calling each of them. I still see these men in my community, and it is water under the bridge now, mainly because someone confronted me about it.

You see, I knew they loved me. They knew me and it gave them license to set me straight. Who do you have to keep you in check? Are you willing to hear it? Or do you just wait for your turn to defend yourself? The answer says a lot about you.

Are you a listener or a talker? I confess to being both. If you're a parent to one of those Teenagers, have you ever seen him or her roll their eyes and say, as you once again try to "teach him in the way he should go," these words? "Oh boy, I feel a lecture coming on." Pretty easy to be the talker, isn't it? How do you react when someone does nothing but preach at you about what *you* should do?

Or what about the times you preach at *yourself* about what you should do? We can squash the power the power of the gifts God has given us when we we repeat misconceptions about ourselves to ourselves. We need the counsel of others. Those who know us fully point out our strengths in ways that we may not see, opening our eyes to the way to pursue our dreams.

The book you are reading is a result of one such relationship in my life. After being subjected to my stories and ways of looking at the world, a leadership coach and mentor encouraged me to write this stuff down. Little did that person know it had always been a goal of mine, and we began talking about what it might look like.

One night my wife and I got together with two other couples we have known for a long time and who are dear to us. The guys were sitting around talking when one of them asked what each of us would do if we just operated in our gifts without respect to income. We decided to answer for one another and to tell them what *we* saw them doing. It might sound like a curious exercise, but it is the example of what I mean—that other people can see us a little more clearly than we can.

One friend said at first that I should coach kids. He had seen me with the baseball teams over the years. He thought I was good with the young men and that I would make a positive impact on them. My other friend said he saw the same qualities in me, but that ultimately, my competitive nature would kill me. Winning the games would eventually eclipse the importance of my wanting to impact the young men's lives, due to my competitive nature. He said coaching was something I should do, but that adults—my peers—people who could hear my message, would be the better audience.

He was dead on. He had the insight into me to speak the truth, because I had allowed him in to see my warts. That conversation led to a seismic shift in my life. I had already been thinking about the coaching aspect that seemed to permeate every area of my life. My work, colleagues, friends, clients, and groups I had led had all been subjected over the years to the message of truth telling and living out loud right in front of them, of confronting issues, feelings, fears and purpose head on. It was where I felt most alive.

Perhaps I would have made that move, including writing this, on my own. But for me, being confirmed by my friends (as we continued talking the other friend agreed) was the last little push I needed to begin fully pursuing my passions. I doubt I would have gone forward with the same conviction and strength of purpose had I not been open enough for them to know me fully.

Hiding can take on and show a very ugly side of our nature if we are not living and feeling in the open. I have been in situations at church where folks have taken time during prayer requests, a time to share burdens and concerns, to gossip about others. ("Let's pray about Jim and his secret drinking problem." After all, it's not gossip if our heads are bowed.) If you have been in that setting, it actually has an unintended humor that would be hard to miss were it not so sad. The truth of it is that those people are hiding behind their own arrogance and want to appear superior for fear that their own mess will be exposed. You know anyone like that?

The judgment that people rain upon one another is the direct result of the same things. We judge, because we hide.

Let's face it. Pointing out the weaknesses in others is much, much easier than the harder work of what I am suggesting. Better to talk about the condition of others than to take the time to actually work on ourselves and our relationships. Doing that requires you to ask the hard questions, and worse, to spend time answering them.

How many times have you been caught in that type of conversation, tearing down someone who is not around? Most of us have done it, and some have perfected the skill.

Here's a saying that may be familiar to you:

> "Great minds discuss ideas.
> Average minds discuss events.
> Small minds discuss people."

Seeking the approval of small-minded people is an impossible task. Don't you know that they are doing the same thing when you are not present? Want to try beginning your life of living in the open? Ask some questions the next time this comes up. Things like, "Would we say these things if this person were around?" Or, "Why do people get pleasure in talking about other people when they aren't around?" Perhaps you will be less popular with a few people, but operating in the open with no agendas will free your heart.

Hiders are everywhere. Posers. People who judge quickly, love superficially, and want to be the center of attention in their feelings of superiority.

I once had a husband and wife come in to review the accounts they had invested through my firm. They were somewhat difficult people, and building a relationship with them had proven to be a challenge. At the end of a meeting with them, I mentioned that I couldn't help but notice the tension that they felt each time we met. The husband then said something that stopped me dead in my tracks.

"Steve, the bottom line is that this money is the most important thing in this world to me."

Said in the presence of his wife of forty-one years, it took my breath away. I could see the hurt in her face, and I instantly knew I could not help them any longer. A strange thing happened for me in that meeting.

I realized he had come out of hiding. I knew where he stood. Was his a warped perspective? Through my eyes, no doubt. But at least I knew where he stood, and I could see clearly the relationship was over.

Wouldn't you just rather know where someone stands? Remember what my son said—rare words of wisdom from a Teenager. "The primary thing that attracts me to someone is that they aren't fake, but that they are a real person."

We will always have people that aren't attracted to our style. Forget pleasing. Be the real one.

My daughter was headed for an interview in a college ministry for a leadership position she had been working toward for several months. She called me on the way to the interview and talked about her nerves, her fear, how it would go. My response was as clear as I have ever delivered.

"Ashley, I have taught you most of what I know. But now you have to live an essential truth, one that will shape everything you do from now on.

"Never be anything other than exactly who you are."

Have you ever been what you thought you were supposed to be, only to get what you were after and then wonder exactly who you are supposed to be now? That now the pressure is on to be who you are *supposed* to be, rather than who you are?

How did that work out for you?

What are you hiding? Who are you hiding from? Is the real you enough? Or is there some flaw you think only *you* have?

When hiding is our standard mode of operation, then coming out from behind the veil and trusting—having faith that who we are is *exactly* enough—is hard work. Indeed, it is the hardest work.

Don't be stalked by that fear any more. You can release all of who you are.

As I once told my wife, "You are so much better than you think you are."

I bet you are, too.

Choose the hard work. Or it will choose you.

On the Road to Real

Do you ever find yourself faking it? _____

If so, how?_____

Where has that gotten you?_____

Are you more attracted to people you see as "faking it" or those who are "the real deal"?_____

Think about this question before answering. What fear is holding you back?

_____

_____

What is your "elephant that is not even there"?

_____

CHAPTER 7

LEARNING WHAT'S IMPORTANT FROM WATCHING POP

"I have come that they may have life, and have it to the full."
—Jesus, in the gospel of John 10:10

"I love you, Boy."

—Pop, spoken repeatedly

"To me, there are three things we all should do every day. We should do this every day of our lives. Number one is laugh. You should laugh every day. Number two is think. You should spend some time in thought. And number three is, you should have your emotions moved to tears, could be happiness or joy. But think about it. If you laugh, you think, and you cry, that's a full day. That's a heck of a day."
—Jim Valvano, Coach and Sportscaster
ESPY Awards Ceremony Speech, 1993

MANY WORDS HAVE been written by many people smarter than me about the condition of the human heart. I guess by now you know I'm not talking about how many times it beats per minute.

I'm talking about our center. I'm talking about the fact that our desire to feel is real.

The heart gives us many things—joy, hurt, love, anger, fulfill-ment, empathy and sympathy, grief, thankfulness, and sadness. You have lived all of these, or you haven't lived long enough. Or do you find yourself not really living at all, but taking care of the things you "must" do? Being a subject to the tyranny of right now?

A full life has lots of stories from the heart, and, as always, I have some stories to tell you. As always, some of those stories are proud family lore and some are, well, things I'm not so proud of. All of them are true, and all of them illustrate why I am who I am. My life feels unlived in parts and gives me a hope for the future, but reflection shows a life that has been lived, nonetheless, sometimes well.

My youth was filled with some common experiences, but some of which one had to grow up out in the country to know.

You also had to have someone like my Pop.

"Pop"—Felton Hammonds Elder, Sr.—was the patriarch of our family in every way. He didn't rule with an iron fist or anything of the sort, but he had lived the kind of life that oozed out of his pores. You didn't spend much time around Pop and not come away knowing you liked him. Unless you let it slip you were a Republican, or anything other than an unabashed lover of the UT Lady Volunteers or New York Yankees.

A man whose formative years were lived during the Depression, he knew what hard times really looked like. We only pretend to know hard times. One of eleven children, Pop saw more change in his ninety years than one can imagine. Flight, the invention of the car, big grocery stores, television, all the things created since 1917. World War II, the rise and fall of communism, and technol-ogy run amok.

And yet, he stayed fully who he was. Change was not something he was terribly interested in. He worked hard at Bruce Flooring, giving part of a finger to it and a lot of sweat. With his labor, he was able to raise a family, squirrel away some money, and farm his land.

Part of that land he gave to my father to build the house my family would grow up in. Down the hill and across the creek (on a bridge he made by hand) from his house was my country won-derland. He raised a large garden, and on our part we kept honey bees and fruit trees. My sister and I picked up walnuts and bagged them to take to the local farmers' co-op for extra money. He taught first my father and then us how to make it, simply by his example. Nothing fancy. Fancy never visited Pop.

The thing he raised best was watermelons. I remember when it was time to pick them how we would go into the garden and he would roll one out, thump it the way farmers know how to do, the way he also taught me. I have picked out more watermelons and cantaloupes at the grocery store by rolling the fruit around and thumping it than I can count. Then he would take out his pocketknife and cut a plug out of the melon to confirm his belief it was ready. After confirmation, we would bust the melon on the ground and eat the heart out of it—that is, the center part that has no seeds—and leave the rest for the birds.

You have not lived until you have eaten the heart out of a watermelon that is warmed by the sun as you stand out in the warm summer air. I didn't stop to say, "Wow, this is great," at the time, but I had the correct sense that life was very, very good.

One summer Pop saw a way for me to earn some extra money. I am sure I helped raise those watermelons, but Pop made me feel like they were all mine. Ultimately, that was his gift. He was about making us feel like we were something more than perhaps we were, but he seemed to have so much conviction in his feelings, you couldn't help but walk with a little more bounce in your step that you were, indeed, special.

One day we loaded up my father's beautiful baby blue 1967 Ford pickup and headed "to town." Our jobs were simple. Pop was the driver and I rode in the back to hawk our melons. My first sales job. I had little idea what I was doing, but Pop made me feel bulletproof.

The part of town Pop drove us into was a mix of ages, but mostly inhabited by country black folks. (And forget the racial stereotyping—I'd bet you a truckload of them that watermelon tastes like summer to people of all races—I know it does to me.)

This neighborhood was an area Pop had grown up taking his own watermelons to for years, and it was his market. When we turned the corner into it and word quickly spread that Mr. Elder had watermelons, people streamed out of their homes to come get one of our prized slices of summer. Within about two hours we had sold a pickup full of watermelons, and I had more money in my pocket than I had ever possessed. To hear Pop tell it, I was the greatest watermelon salesman you have ever seen, and he would have happily told you about it until the day he died. Why, you should have seen the way I had people eating out of my hands!

A small thing, but a very large thing to a boy in those awkward early teenage years. He had the gift of letting me know how special *he* thought I was, and that was enough. My heart was full of pride. I was not just good, I was great. I only hope to live to see the day when I can have the same impact on my grandchildren.

Come to think of it, I hope to have that impact on my children. They are nineteen and sixteen as I'm writing this book. Isn't it funny how we always look to the future and our hopes for it, but we walk right by what is straight away in front of us?

I want someone to say about me what I had the privilege of saying about my Pop, and really, really felt, the sad day we said our final goodbye to him.

Here is what I said about him at his funeral:

> I am humbled to be here to talk about what Pop taught and gave me during his life, and I feel like a little kid when I see all the Elder family here. One of my favorite speeches ever was given by Jim Valvano at the end of his life, where he said that there are three things we must do to live a full day. We should take the time to think, we should have our emotions moved to tears, and we should laugh. These last few days have certainly provided us with plenty of time to think, and our emotions have been moved an awful lot. We have laughed, and we have cried.
>
> First was Pop's English. He mangled words a lot and was especially fond of messing up athletes' names. When I was growing up, we liked to drink Sprite and took it with us to baseball games. Pop called it "Sprout." When I was a teenager,

Jim Plunkett won the Super Bowl with the Raiders and Pop was a fan of his, always talking about the way that "Puckett" could throw the ball. And perhaps the greatest female basketball player ever for the Lady Vols, Chamique Holdsclaw, was known only to us via Pop as "Coleslaw." We used to put all these together in a sentence and ask him if "Puckett and Coleslaw was drinking them some Sprout."

The second thing was something Pop and I had in common. I would highly recommend you not acquiring one of these, but we, amazingly, had the same finger on the same hand cut off in the same place. Mine was cut off in my wreck, and I was quite upset about this. But Pop came into my hospital room and offered to show me that there were things I could do with that finger that others could only dream of. Now, I will not show you what that is, but if you would like to see me afterwards, I would be happy to share. We got a good laugh out of it, and I have shared this trick with preschool kids in church, much to their parents' horror.

Third were his political and baseball allegiances. Pop was a Democrat and a Yankees fan. I grew up to be a Red Sox fan and a Republican. This was a great disappointment to Pop. Every phone call I would throw in something about how good the Red Sox were and how great it was to be a Republican. He would generally say some things that were not so nice. It all culminated ten days ago, the last time I got to see Pop. He struggled throughout my time with him, but he had a few minutes where I could really understand him at the end of my visit. He said "Boy, let me tell you something." Now when he said that, he generally meant business, and knowing this might be the last time I ever talked with him, I leaned in, thinking something profound might be coming. He then said, "George Bush is the worst damn President we ever had."

The man loved biscuits. It is his fault I look like this. You know the man could eat when his brother, my Great Uncle Tinky, sat me down the night of visitation and said, "Did he ever tell you how many biscuits he could eat as a kid?" He confirmed for me the stories Pop had told me about being at the table with his parents and all his brothers and sisters, and the whole table had just stopped to watch him eat. He loved to put Bob White syrup over them and everything else. I would clear out the shelves whenever I could find it, and the last time I got to bring him some, he ate fourteen bottles in just over a month. I asked if they had it in IV bags, but no luck.

Pop had a gift. He just made me feel special. Only later in life did I realize that was true of everyone he loved. When I was a kid, we picked watermelons he had raised and filled Dad's truck up and went to town to sell them. He made me out to be the greatest watermelon seller of all time. It makes for a cute story now, but it was a big deal to a fourteen-year-old kid.

And he taught me how to head a family. Not through money, or titles, or a resume, but a life of love. In the thirteenth chapter of 1 Corinthians, Paul begins with "I will now show you the most excellent way" and ends it with, "And now these three remain: Faith, Hope and Love. But the greatest of these is Love."

Pop didn't preach through loud sermons, but through his life. I saw a quote once that said "Preach continuously. Use words if necessary." That sums up Pop's life pretty well.

First as a grandfather to my cousin Melinda, my sister Sandy and me, along with six great grandchildren. Melinda said when we had family prayer last night that it was an honor to be his grandchild, and it was. I had two dads—but Pop was the perfect one because he wasn't burdened with the weight of having to discipline me. Pop would say from time to time, "Your Dad is being too hard on you, you just hang in there." When things weren't going particularly well at home, I would share that pearl of wisdom with my Dad, and that would not go over too well, as you might imagine. Dad would then tell me, "Let me tell you who he was to your Aunt Jo and I when we were growing up."

As a father, first to my Dad, who loved, provided, disciplined, and coached me. He poured his life out for Sandy and me. All things he learned from Pop.

Then to Pop's daughter, my Aunt Jo. She raised her own family in love and motherly concern. Her marriage to Uncle Bill has produced another beautiful family in Melinda and Doug along with their two wonderful daughters. Personally, she helped nurse me after my wreck for five months after my mom had to go back to work, with no though of what she would get in return. . . all things she learned from Pop.

And as a husband of sixty-eight years and nine months to our Mammie. He loved her, cherished her, and longed to be with her to his very end. He and Mammie prayed for, by name, his whole family. "And the two became one flesh," the great truth the Bible promises. So we men learned from him how to love our wives as Christ loved the church. We all learned to love deeply.

My sister Sandy said it best. As we were talking before coming to the funeral, she said, "I just cannot imagine a world without Pop." And even though he is staring at the face of his Savior, and I know he is . . .

If it feels like we have lost a piece of ourselves . . . it is because we have.

And if it feels like we have lost a hero . . . it is because we have.

Standing up there to talk about Pop was one of the more emotional moments of my life, and the hardest thing I have ever had to speak. But it was also one of the greatest privileges, because I didn't have to dig to say something nice about him.

So there's Pop's legacy, what he has left behind. And now, I beg you to entertain this question. Are you on track to have Pop's story be the end of your story? To have such love surrounding you as you depart this world?

Or are you on the train track straight to some other place? People will miss you, sure, but, well, you just haven't made the impact you wanted to.

And then this. What are you going to do about it?

On the Road to Real

Right now, what do you think will be your legacy? What would you leave behind *today*?

What do you want to leave behind?

_____

_____

Is there a gap between the two? _____

If so, what action can you take to close that gap?

_____

_____

_____

CHAPTER 8

THE BITTERNESS BATTLE

Bitterness imprisons life; love releases it. Bitterness paralyzes life; love empowers it. Bitterness sickens life; love heals it. Bitterness blinds life; love anoints its eyes.

— Harry Emerson Fosdick

Let all bitterness, wrath, anger, clamor, and evil speaking be put away from you.

— the apostle Paul in the New Testament book of Ephesians 4:31

GETTING OLDER IS a lot like riding a rollercoaster. After your body realizes what it has just been through, you throw up.

My wife and I went through a huge organizational project recently. We had neglected to organize or frame twenty–two years' worth of pictures—maybe thousands of them. Stretching all the way back to our honeymoon, they were stored in several large boxes in no particular order. We decided to get them in order.

As you read about our project, your first thought might be— what a wonderful stroll through memories, kids growing up, small treasures of love growing up to be teenagers, trips taken. Precious, to be sure. But for me, something else came into sharp focus.

I am aging. Getting old. . . er. My body has changed. My hair has grayed—make that turned white. My eyes show the telltale signs of too much worry, not quite enough rest, and a little too much of enjoying the finer things of life.

This realization hits us all, and there are many redeeming things about enjoying the fruits of our labor, of different stages of life, new dreams to be dreamed.

I have noticed, however, a shocking thing about my peers, and generally about a lot of my clients at or past retirement age.

Bitterness has crept in. The prism through which they see the world has turned decidedly negative. Time is spent not on things that give energy, but on those things that take our energy away. Endless talk radio or 24/7 news channels with their neverending pundits, and loops over and over of the same footage on every subject from politics to the financial markets to scandal. Their news is filled with the horrors of murder, crime, scandal—the very worst humanity has to offer. News and the media have to "sell it" to us to keep us close, and we have bought it.

Life, when lived long enough, will kick us in the teeth. The dreams of our youth will evaporate. Nothing looks quite like what we thought it would. We had all the answers, only to discover (drum roll). . .that we had no answers. We just make it up as we go along.

A colleague at work speculated with me that many things lead down this path. Marriages go bad, business begins to weaken, relationships become harder and take real work, and our youth has escaped us. What is really left?

So we decide to unplug from the world. I went through a time where I was so sick of talking by the time I got to the end of my work day that I came home and just wanted to disconnect. Don't bother me with the challenges the kids face. No, I don't want to talk about my day. I want to watch ESPN and see what is next. Entertain me. I just finished work and now I deserve to just sit here and let time go by.

We need rest, and God only knows how much simpler we need to make our lives. In fact, He tells us this repeatedly, but we get so busy we forget to listen.

There are different kinds of rest. The restoring value of true rest is a wonderful thing and we need it in this noisy world we created. Take it. Engineer times to have it. Read, relax, enjoy those you love. But destructive so-called rest, or what we want to excuse by calling it "rest" is really laziness justified. Unplugging from the world in a harsh, stand-the-line way is an invitation to our true enemy.

Isolation. Loneliness. The sum of our lives is nothing more than the small choices we make every day, and as our energy gets sapped away, we choose to. . . do nothing.

Leave me alone! Those three words become our rallying cry, and we run to be entertained. We switch on the talking heads, tune out, and sink down into the recliner once again, listening to the latest sensational "Breaking News"—and it's all "breaking news"—with a celebrity's divorce getting as much—no, more—coverage than a major offensive by our military. Example: When CNN recently aired a talk show about Michael Jackson, the banner at the bottom of the screen read, "BREAKING NEWS: Michael Jackson is Dead." This was *five days* after he had died.

Thanks for that up-to-the-minute breaking news. Really.

If we let them, the constant sensationalism, and what is really not much more than noise, will follow us to our graves.

We're so used to tuning out the background noise that we can miss hearing the music of life. Let me give you a story of an almost missed opportunity: My wife and I recently were invited to a night at the symphony. Now normally, it would not fire us up to drive forty-five minutes from home for a couple hours' entertainment, but a few things drew us in. In Nashville, Music City, there is a new ar-chitectural marvel and a crown jewel for the city. The Schermerhorn Symphony Hall, widely held to be one of the best in the world is right here in Tennessee. Vince Gill, he with the voice of an angel, was going to sing with the full symphony, and the opportunity to see friends we see too little of all enticed us to say yes.

When the day rolled around, how do you think we talked about it? "The weather is cold and disgusting." "We won't get back until really late." "I don't want to get ready." These and other complaints ruled our conversation. But we had said yes, so on we rolled.

We had a phenomenal meal and wonderful fellowship with our friends. Nicole Kidman was seated right beside us, but it was a girl's night out for her and her friends, so she was without her husband, Keith Urban, to our wives' eternal dismay. The symphony played stunningly, Vince Gill was spellbinding, and that building's own music spoke to everyone who was there. I will never forget Vince turning off all the house microphones so we could "hear the instrument this building is" as he sang "Threaten Me With Heaven." It was perhaps the most beautiful thing I have ever heard.

When it was over, we marveled at what a wonderful time we had. And we thought back to our conversation earlier that day. What were we thinking? There was a time when we would have given no thought to not going. What had happened?

Our lives were so filled with the demands of the day, with the overwhelming demands adulthood places on us, that our desire to unplug almost robbed us of a wonderful experience and time with our friends. We just wanted to lie there. If we had not gone? Pajamas, maybe a movie on cable if it was a big night, talk of how tired we were—those things would have ruled the night. Where is the life in that?

Let's take an aerial shot of what life looks like at this fork in the road. Kind of a 10,000-foot flyover that removes you from the distractions for a moment.

Do you have a relationship in your life that you avoid at all costs? A parent, grandparent, friend that you dread seeing, talking to on the phone, that you have to be around on holidays? That sucks the very life out of you?

Now back to earth. Alongside you, I doubt this person's attitude toward life is one you'd choose for yourself. When we remove ourselves a bit and see the effect in someone else of what we are also choosing, we see clearly what we *don't* want to become. So what do we do about it?

Or, if given the choice, do you wish to be that other person you also surely know, full of energy, full of life? Who has an optimism that others feed off? Who always seems to have a spare hand to help, who *chooses* to love people, who always has an ear to hear your troubles?

Choose people. Choose community. Create the community you want. Get out and nourish relationships that are going to take you along, that will nourish you. Be with "nutritious people," with those who teach us if we will just be quiet and listen, who will share our burdens as we also share theirs. "He ain't heavy, he's my brother"— or sister. Partners in living, that's what we all need. Sometimes we aren't even strong enough to prop up ourselves, And there will be times when you will be the one to prop them up.

So. . .isolation is our enemy, and choosing to connect will keep that enemy locked out. That's one down. Here's another enemy we need to give the boot to.

It's called "settling." We've settled. Somewhere, we have settled.

We strive for comfort, and we lose our way. Carving out our own little piece of heaven, or what we think is our heaven, we lose the ability to live. We become about ourselves. Our tolerance level for anything that makes us uncomfortable, that gets us out of the little cocoon we've spun around ourselves? Well, that just won't do.

I've noticed something pretty interesting when I've looked up at the bleachers at the many baseball, football, and basketball games I have been to and coached. Take a look around. How many grandparents do you see there? We always had just one set of grandparents who showed up no matter the temperature, the time, or the place. They were there for their grandchild, and had made it a priority in their lives.

Sure, we have things to do, and as we get older we have earned the right to a little "me" time. But I never really understood why those two grandparents were the only ones there. Some live out of town, and some have passed on, but many live right under their children's and grandchildren's noses and just choose not to be there. They have something better to do, something they want to do. And I don't mean occasionally, I mean all the time.

My grandfather never missed a game I played. One of the comforting sights of my growing up years was looking down one of the outfield lines and seeing him sitting in his lawn chair. He was a constant in my life. I always drew great comfort from him just being there. He didn't have to have some great pearl of wisdom if I didn't play well or my team lost. Just being present was enough.

Now this isn't just about attendance at ball games. It is a symptom of how we tend to *not* choose relationship. I will tell you what all those hot summer days and nights earned my Pop. He had my ear. He cared enough to show up and it built the foundations of a relationship I will carry with me until I die, and if I am blessed enough to watch my grandchildren at play, I will show up. I want to be their Pop, not some figurehead who is supposed to be loved just because he shows up on holidays.

I choose to be engaged. Do you think there aren't things that don't drive me absolutely crazy about my kids, even occasionally my wife and my friends? Of course. Am I going to trot out my mental checklist of them? Nope. Instead, I will focus on a key truth. I am no piece of cake to be around sometimes, and I am betting you aren't, either.

Get outside yourself. Take a flyover and look at yourself. All that negativity you are giving off is killing your chances at a full life. But it's not anything that some fresh air and being with people you love won't cure.

Choose them.

On the Road to Real

Do you find your thoughts getting more negative as time ticks away?

Are there relationships right in your face you aren't pursuing? Why is that?

_____

_____

What happens to your negative thoughts when you are actively doing the things and engaged with the people you love?

_____

_____

What can you do today to pursue those things?

_____

What will you do today to choose people?

_____

_____

_____

CHAPTER 9

THE SIMPLER MIND

I am not interested in my players' evaluation of me. I am interested in my evaluation of them. That's what I get paid to do.
> —Pittsburgh Steelers Coach Mike Tomlin,
> responding to a question regarding what
> he thought of a player's praise of him.

I wish I had an answer for that, because I am tired of hearing that question.
> —Yogi Berra

STRONG LEADERSHIP. IT requires guts, determination, foresight, and never letting them see you sweat.

Doesn't that statement make you tired even to read it?

There is a time for all of that. Showing strength, leading our families, making a business work, being married, doing all of the right things.

But I have a sense that most of us walking around every day have something else in common that is holding us back.

We. Are. Very. Tired.

The demands of adulthood are, simply put, overwhelming at times. All of the things talked about in previous chapters that you know firsthand.

We give our kids, friends, spouses, jobs, churches, communities, and our blind ambitions all that we are. Sometimes it becomes good enough to just get out of bed and show up—it's all we've got left.

On a conference call with other advisors recently, six of us who are involved in a consulting and coaching program were doing an annual review of our businesses and what had transpired over that year. The stock market had been brutal, and our economy seemed to be in a death spiral.

The first team to speak seemed to have run like a well-greased machine. They had implemented every program, every process imaginable that had been borne out of all the previous sessions, and every goal they set for their practice had been hit. The markets were seemingly just a sideshow, for it had little impact on their performance, attitude, or results.

Now many others have written the book about that kind of performance. About not letting obstacles get in their way. I personally want to know their secrets. All valid, and something we who strive to improve need to know.

If you haven't figured it out, this is not that book.

I am far more interested in the next team that reported. While the team of power was reporting, I sat on the other end of that call, embarrassed. My report was going to sound nothing like them. We had made improvements, yet had been sidetracked by the events of the day. Clients were in freak-out mode, and our office had become more of a psychology ward than an advisory practice.

While I was trying to craft what I would say when it was my turn, the next team was asked where they stood. Their spokesperson's response changed everything.

"You have got to be freaking kidding me." Silence. "It is all I can do to drag my butt out of bed every day."

Immediately, "amens" started sounding from various points on the call. One advisor chimed in, "Thank you for being honest. I feel the same way." He went on. Talked about his hurt, fear, the pain he was living in. The doubt—about everything—that had crept into everything he was doing, and his worry that systems had fallen by the way side as a vast forest fire engulfed him and his practice.

So what happened? It didn't turn into a complaining session. It just simply was people sharing their hearts, talking out loud about all the things they had been scared to say when the call started and admitting they were not helped by the fact that the first team to speak evidently possessed superpowers.

These were not run-of-the-mill people on this call. We are talking about high achievers, people who saw it through failures—hungry, hardworking folks.

But they were all overwhelmed. And they needed to talk. That one hour phone call freed hearts.

Don't you find yourself needing some of that kind of freedom?

So how do we find it?

First, we need to give ourselves a break. We talk to ourselves. And we are not so nice. Have you listened to *you* lately?

I have come to believe the difference between the team that had it all together and everyone else on that call is that the team who had met the goals was operating in a peaceful place. They are working in their *calling*, and they know it. Peace *was* their process. They were in control as a result. The rest of us? We were swimming upstream and facing headwinds we were not prepared for, while struggling against the current so violently that fighting the rapids became our purpose. No one had thought to stop and take account. To call time-out, lift the oars into the canoe, and float awhile.

I once heard a man say, "A quiet mind renders peace . . . and performance." So how do we get there, to a simpler, quieter mind?

What I am about to say goes against every self-help book ever written and flies in the face of every "pull yourself up and keep on fighting" piece of advice you have ever heard.

Stop. Now.

Call time-out. You have some saving to do, and it is of yourself.

Perhaps you are operating in your purpose, your calling right now. You are in the minority.

Not long ago when I was the guest speaker to some young couples at church, during the question and answer portion of my time a young lady laid out her situation for me. She and her husband had managed every nickel and still found themselves in a constant state of scarcity. It still wasn't enough.

There was a time in my life when I would have tried to come up with a solution, a way to tighten that budget even more, to help her fix her problem. What came out of my mouth next spoke to the truth of the time-out.

"If, indeed, you are getting all you can out of your resources and still find it is not enough, maybe your problem is not in what you spend. You just aren't making enough money."

Now I know, sometimes we are limited by our training, education, the economic circumstances surrounding us. But do we ever step back and question—do we ever objectively take a look at our situation? Or do we wallow in the mud of thoughts like, "This is just the way it is, and it is not fun?"

How is the way you are doing things now working for you? Are you tired, sick of it, working nonstop at home or in your job? How about your health and fitness? Maybe it's not what it should be. And God only knows you wouldn't want anyone to be able to read the thoughts going through that brain of yours.

How is that working for you?

Stop. Now.

Bagger Vance had this figured out. As Rannulph Junuh's caddy, he was teaching him everything but golf. He was teaching him how to live. After the first of four rounds in his match, Junuh had embarrassed himself and found himself already twelve shots behind—a mind-boggling deficit to overcome, especially against the great Jones and Hagen. As he stood on the first tee, his demons having fully shown themselves in the morning round, Junuh was like so many of us. He showed up because he had to, but was full of fear and self-doubt, knowing people were talking about his inadequacies. Before he could hit his first shot, Bagger had some wisdom to give him. Only out of his desperation—only because of his pain, having fallen flat on his face already—could Junuh open his ears and hear. His pain led him to grab onto Bagger's words:

> "Watch Bobby Jones over there. He is swinging with his own authentic swing. There's a perfect shot out there for each and every one of us, and all we got to do is to get ourselves out of its way—let it choose us. I can't take you there, Junuh. I just hopes I can help you find the way."

Is the only thing in your way . . . you?

Learn to say no. The season of yes will come. But first, the season of no.

It will not be easy. You will feel the mother of all tripwires, guilt. We are so conditioned to jerking ourselves around at every turn, of doing all the things we have to do, that we will not enter into this time easily or without an internal fight.

I would say this, too: Keep it personal. Do it for yourself. Tell your spouse or one person close to you. Start with just a day. Drop off the grid, so to speak. Sit in silence and grab a book. Have a pen and pad ready. The thoughts will flood to you. Write them all down, all the craziness that has enveloped your mind, creating a fog that you haven't had headlights strong enough to see through.

Confusion is the enemy. Getting all that stuff out of your head is your only hope. And you cannot do any of it with Oprah or the stock-market channel providing the soundtrack of noise.

Airplanes don't take off in that kind of fog. How do you expect to live the life you hoped for when you don't even know—can't even see—what your hopes are?

When I had my accident, I went from carefree to just trying to survive. The reason that led to my twilight zone was that I never shifted out of that survival mode. I didn't try to see my way through the fog that blew in with the loss of my previous identity. Instead, I began reacting to the pain, trying to mask it, trying not to care that the fog threatened to keep the real me in the shadows. I turned to drugs, alcohol, anything to numb me from feeling lost.

The truth behind that shift was fear. Who was I now? Would people accept me? Would anyone really love me? What did I have? Was I worthy of friends, of relationships, of anything?

The choices many of us make now to numb us may not be as evil in themselves as drugs and alcohol can be, but they can act in the same manner, like a quick coat of cheap paint over a table that really needs the bare wood sanded down and exposed first. We shop, we spend, we accumulate, we seek the love and approval of others, and we look for power anywhere we can find it, be it the board room or PTA meeting. But those quick fixes don't take care of the underlying need.

These days we are missing a key component of my Pop's life, indeed something of a day gone swiftly past. When I would drive home from classes or work in high school, I had to pass his house as we slowed to turn into our driveway. Unless it was cold, each afternoon, Pop was sitting on the front porch in his chair. Just sitting, thinking, watching the world, relaxing. He would often comment on what a hurry the world seemed to be in, how fast everyone was going.

When is the last time you had some "porch time"? Although the outdoor air, the birds singing, trees blowing in the wind always stirs me, porch time can be anywhere you deem it to be. Just turn down the volume. Escape for a few hours to a place just for you, and *begin*. Reclaim yourself. Surrender what imprisons you.

And say no. The yes that waits for you will be bigger than you imagined.

On the Road to Real

Challenge: Take a work day off *just for you*. Spend time in silence, with no television, no BlackBerry. Go on a technology strike to see what silence feels like and what will happen. Grab a pen and a tablet and write down the thoughts that come. Write them all down and get them out. You can never get started unless you *get started*.

Below are some questions to help you get your fog lights on. You cannot move forward unless you address them. They'll help you begin to see through the fog, rather than just feeling lost, dazed, and confused. I encourage you to take time to grab that pen and paper so you can jot down answers, thoughts, questions, and fears. This information is for your eyes only—so be honest with yourself.

What is it I am so worried about? Exactly?

What am I striving for? Am I striving for anything?

What is my purpose?

Is that enough for me?

What did I dream of 10 years ago?

Is it dead now? Still viable?

What am I doing for ME?

What am I saying NO to?

What am I saying YES to?

Do I feel passion about those things?

CHAPTER 10

KNOWING
WHO YOU ARE

When I was a child, I talked like a child, I thought like a child, I reasoned like a child. When I became a man, I put childish ways behind me.

—1 Corinthians 13:11

"The only difference between that old preacher and me was that he worked for God and *I am God*!"

—Robert DeNiro as Chief "Billy" Sunday
in *Men of Honor*

"I'm a man without conviction
I'm a man who doesn't know. . .
Karma karma karma karma karma chameleon. . . "

—Boy George and the Culture Club, 1984

CULTURE.
A word difficult to define, yet with so many meanings. . . and answers.

I'm pretty sure Boy George's Culture Club was a product of a different culture than mine. So what is mine? What is yours?

Ask what "culture" is in the South and you are going to hear cries of "Southern by the grace of God." And we mean it. If you have ever spent any time here, you know why.

We love our college football. And we love southern food so good it is its own tradition—"dinner-on-the-grounds" recipes like chess pie and made-from-scratch butter cake, our sweet tea and our fried chicken, and the staff of life, the Almighty Biscuit.

"Yes, sir" and "Yes, Ma'am" are beaten into us from the time we are old enough to speak. If you don't acknowledge your elders in that way, you either did not have proper raisin' or you are a spoiled brat. And your name is Preston Trueblood VII or some such ridiculous Yankee name.

Our culture has its ugly baggage. The Civil War and slavery come to mind.

On the positive side, we have southern girls, barbecue, and the best music in the United States—no, the world. We have Music City, the World's Largest Fish Fry, the Strawberry Festival, Mule Day, the Loveless Café, Beale Street, the Natchez Trace, and the World's Longest Yard Sale. And SEC football. Can't forget that.

We know who we are.

And that is one powerful piece of information.

As a nation of people, it seems these days we *don't* know who we are. As I write this, we have just witnessed the inauguration of our first African American President. Barack Obama has given the country hope in a time when we desperately need all we can get our hands on as a country. Appears to me he won the election in part because he could bring people together, help us forge a common identity, and repair the fractured—or shattered—culture that our country has become.

Wherever you are from, you grew up with people that to outsiders seem to possess certain unmistakable characteristics. If you are from the South and you go to Boston, you're likely to think, "People from the Northeast talk funny and go really fast." If you head out to California you might think everyone there seems friendly and laid-back—that is, until you have driven on the L.A. highways, an experience that will crush that myth in less time than it would take you to move over to one of the Santa Monica Freeway's jammed exit ramps during rush hour.

Culture. Companies talk a lot about "the culture" they strive to create. Some are quite good at walking the talk. But many simply write a mission statement because they are supposed to, and it is nothing more than a guiding principle they *wish* they stood for and can trot out for their annual shareholders' meetings or to put in their annual statements. The real culture is centered around making all the money the company can. People are nothing more than a vehicle to get the company to that destination.

Culture. Each home has its own, too. You can tell the story of your being brought up, and it is different from mine, and probably your best friend's. In our house, when it's time to make a decision about something, I'm apt to say, "It's trigger-pullin' time"—Did I mention I am a Southerner? You may also have little family jokes, sayings, or ways of doing things that no other family has. That's your culture.

You are creating culture around you through the people you love, whether you know it or not. People are watching you. If you have children, you can forget sometimes, because as they become teenagers they seem to have one goal, and that is to get away from you. Or so they would have you think. They still really need you. More than ever. It is just a secret they cannot even communicate.

If you are married, you and your spouse create the culture of your life together. Your story is there to be written. What are you creating? A life together full of love and experience, or are you just getting by, making ends meet, going through the motions?

Within our circle of friends we create together a culture of bond, an attachment. Through shared beliefs, hobbies, and interests, through our children's friendships and activities, and in our working hours, we are attracted to people to form sometimes Providential relationships that help shape our lives. For we cannot do it alone.

But we try. Boy, do we try.

Our common culture now is one of—and here is the great rub—one of secrets. We pose. We want the smiles and the laughs and the money earned, but we don't want to get at the hard truths.

God only knows we don't want anyone to know our secrets, the unspoken things in all our hearts that act as boogers on the soul.

Well, let's talk about how to pick those suckers.

My great shaping in this area took place in a men's Bible study. Five guys who didn't all know one another were brought together by my friend Gary. He had played golf with each of us at different times, and he felt the call to bring us together. The confluence of events that led each of us to say "yes" to getting together with strangers and talking about personal subjects is still astounding.

We met with good intentions for about a year and a half every Friday morning. As with most adults who have their lives squarely in their rear-view mirror, trusting each other and letting our guard down did not come natural to us. We grew closer through our new shared bond, but we just skimmed the surface enough to have something stirred up in us.

And then the bottom fell out. My childish days were coming to an end.

One day I was sitting in church listening to the preacher get started. I had begun leading a class at church that was well attended and that people seemed to enjoy. Leadership had found me within the church. I was striving so much to appear the good Christian, and was feeling growth in my relationship with God. I was serving in several capacities within that body and my reputation was growing.

I had everyone fooled. Bankruptcy, acting like a fool, acting like a child. That was the real me, and no one knew the full story. There were good things about me, but no one knew the whole enchilada, and all of a sudden the check came due. I knew the bill had to be paid. I could no longer go on living behind any type of façade.

I never heard a word the preacher said. A lightning bolt hit me. Something I had never felt before cut into my soul. I was pierced. And there was no escape.

I was a conflicted fraud. A flat-out liar in some ways. I was broke in every way. Both financially and morally, I was a train wreck looking for a car to plow into. And I could not get away from the coming disaster.

There were good aspects in my life, to be sure. But have you ever gotten to a place in your life when you were stuck, and you knew that in order to move forward some things had to be dealt with? You may have gone far and achieved at a high level in your career while keeping your reputation intact, but deep down you felt like you were fooling people.

The voice in the lightning bolt said that, for me, it was time to 'fess up.

I was scared out of my mind. I am talking about my-feet-are-sweating, get-me-out-of-here fear. I wish it were a panic attack. That would have been so easy, so explainable. But, no, my time of reckoning had come. Check, please! It was time to pay up.

After a miserable day, I got to work the next day. I had a calendar full of commitments. I canceled all of them and made the phone call.

"Gary, I need to come see you. Right now."

I don't know what I would have done had he said no. Instead, he greeted me with a willing but hesitant voice.

I drove to his house like a man who has not eaten in a year who knows the person he's going to see has fresh biscuits with something awful like cottage cheese baked into them waiting for him. He's so hungry he thinks he wants them, but he also dreads them. But he needs them. I was that guy.

When I got there, Gary asked me to hold up before I spoke. He told me he had prayed and asked for someone to show himself to him, a person on whom he could unload a serious burden he had been carrying. Stunned, I proceeded with my story of shame, guilt, hurt, and fear. He responded with his own.

It was in that moment we realized a great truth. We are not alone in this battle. And we need fellow soldiers. We need to lift up and support each other.

The events that followed were not clean. I would love to report that we walked away, felt better, and moved on.

The truth is much messier.

I went through a time of true hurt. For the first time in my life, I realized just how much my actions had hurt me, the ones

I love, and the ones that trusted in me. I had been a very selfish, childish man, and the time to put childish things behind me had come, indeed.

Confession time with Gary was a great start. After a time of serious internal debate, I had to confront the truth that if I was to stay married to my wife, she had to really know me. All of me. All I had done, some at serious cost to her. Pain she did not deserve.

This newfound freedom was hard fought. I had to come to grips with who I was and with what I had made.

Without question, there are consequences in our actions. Mine was the initial shame and guilt that I needed, desired, to feel. I had earned it. My wife chose to walk down the path with me.

So again I say the process to which I invite you is one that involves some initial pain. The hiding, the posing, the *being* who we think others expect us to be is a heavy burden when not fully supported by the truth. You get on the train to success as you have defined it, but somewhere the train becomes a runaway one. The dream you once created outgrew and got ahead of your character, your personal development, and your maturity. And you find yourself in a place of feeling as though the world is about to catch onto you.

For me, it was the beginning. Inflicting pain on people is no fun, and many of us do it unintentionally, without thought. We hurt those we love the most through our emptiness—because we give all our energy and focus to our jobs, careers, churches, and communities. But we forget to take care of ourselves and our families first, and by the time we turn our attention to them, we're bled dry—"I gave at the office"—and there's nothing left to give. We don't build the right priority list; we just chase. We are afraid of getting left behind, that the world will not stop, that we will miss opportunity if we take time to collect ourselves and ask the hard questions.

I made what perhaps was the most difficult decision of all: to engage in a process. Now hear that. *Process.* This is not an overnight phenomenon. As difficult as the first steps are, what follows is a time of commitment. We change in the way we think, we reprioritize what we value, and we begin to tell the truth. I made the decision to get comfortable in my own skin. And it didn't happen immediately.

But it did begin to happen, and for me the results were palpable. At that time, my wife of fifteen years began to really know me fully for the first time. We had loved one another, had children, had some fun, and had stayed married. But for the first time she began to know me, warts and all. I stopped being the loudest and most opinionated in my circle of friends. I quit a lot of commitments that I had taken on. I didn't withdraw, but I began taking time to work on me, to make sure that everything in my life was genuine and that it reflected my true passion and calling for that time. I began the process of making sure I would never do or say yes to anything that was going to get less than all of me.

I chose to be present when I said I was going to be. Not just there, but engaged. I had a family that needed a full-time me, not a me who was worried about what was over my shoulder, who was chasing. . .always chasing. Or running. Running from the possibility that maybe, just maybe, I was not fully who I said I was.

I vowed to be true.

Where do you come from? How far have you strayed from who you really are? For many, that is a question always in the back of our minds. We know who we are, what our root system is. Are the turns that we have chosen in our lives genuine and true to that?

I come from a family of four that got its roots from my Pop's family. Pop was one of eleven children and the third of six sons. Pop's family wasn't perfect to be sure, but my great grandparents' main aim in life was to provide in every way for their family. That family was rooted in a tradition that taught they weren't too high and mighty to do hard work of any kind. They were farmers, but they'd pick cotton for someone else when no other work was available—they were made of honest, straight-ahead stuff.

Still hanging on the back of my Pop's house is a dinner bell that belonged to his parents. Granny Elder would come out and ring that bell twice a day at lunch and dinner to let the men know that it was time to eat and work was to be stopped out in the fields. Cooking for a family of that size, including the hired hands who helped on the farm, was a monumental chore on which she worked nonstop.

During that time, corn meal was much less expensive than flour. All the children would watch as Granny prepared mountains of homemade biscuits at every meal, and when the meal was on the table, she would use the still hot oven to make huge cast iron skillets of corn bread, which would be . . . thrown to the dogs. The humans got biscuits—cornbread was dog food. My Pop never ate cornbread.

When your blood comes from such a rich place as this, how can you ever stray too far from it?

And yet I had. Honesty had not been the cornerstone of my life. I was chasing an image—what other people thought I needed to be. I even allowed myself to be coached on what kind of car I should drive. Ever had that conversation with someone? We are so image conscious. Have you, like me, ever thought more about the statement your car makes than what it is that really drives and hides in your soul?

I drive a little pickup truck now. Bought new a decade ago. I am emotionally attached to it. I have coached baseball out of it for ten years and have had "the birds and the bees talk" with my son on the way to a baseball tournament in it. We have laughed, cried, fought, and shared stories in that truck.

And yet, being in the business of handling people's money, I hear comments all the time. "When you going to get a new truck?" "How long you gonna drive that thing?" Guess they think a banged-up old pickup is not the appropriate vehicle of choice for a financial planner. Know what? I don't care anymore.

As I drive my little truck, it drives home for me some commonsense advice to myself: Don't forget where you come from. Stay humble. That truck says a little about who I am, I hope. It's kept me from turning again into someone who is so image conscious he will go through his life faking it, being someone he doesn't even really like to impress other people he doesn't really know with money he doesn't have.

I choose to know me, to have others know me, and to walk around being true to what and who I am, staying close to my roots.

I want those who love me to say about me what I said about my Pop at his funeral.

I choose biscuits. Leave the dog food for someone else.

On the Road to Real

How would you describe your roots and the culture you come from?

_____

_____

Have you ever felt like you were not being totally honest with others about yourself?

_____

Have you ever felt like you were faking it? When and how?

_____

_____

If you could do one thing now to leave childish ways behind, what would it be?

_____

_____

Make a promise to yourself to do it.

CHAPTER 11

THE BEST THINGS IN LIFE AREN'T THINGS

Friendship is born at that moment when one person says to another, 'What! You too? I thought I was the only one.'

—C. S. Lewis, *The Four Loves*

The highlight of my childhood was making my brother laugh so hard that food came out of his nose.

—Garrison Keillor

I LIVE IN the Bible belt. I am a Christian, and that is the way I see the world.

I grew up in church, and as we say in the South, "I had a drug problem. If the doors were open at church, my parents drug me to church."

I am now in a church we love, and it is one of the ways my wife and I have chosen our community and our culture.

If you haven't figured this out by now, just because you're in my community doesn't mean I won't make fun of you. No one on this earth is untouchable, including—especially including—me.

I have seen some of the funniest things you can imagine at church. I've learned that no church is perfect, because it has people in it—including me.

East Union Baptist Church was where my parents dragged me. I even enjoyed it from time to time. Brother Calvin Moore was the preacher there until recently. I liked Brother Calvin. He could get fired up as only a good country preacher can. He was also a farmer on the side, and I would see him driving his tractor up and down our road doing various chores, turning someone's garden over for them and the like.

I also liked the fact he only had two good fingers. The rest of them were cut off in various places in some terrible accident or another. But that didn't stop him from doing anything, from preaching to playing softball.

We had good old-fashioned traditions in that church. Potluck suppers were aplenty. Chitlin dinners were a somewhat regular event. If you don't know what a *chitlin* is, I will spare you the great details, but here are the two things I know about them. These fine pieces of eatin' were hog intestines, and they were supposedly washed down real good before some person with more "intestinal fortitude" than I had threw them in a pot and cooked them.

I never ate chitlins.

My sense of humor began to be sharpened in that sanctuary. Being a small country church, our choir would not remind you of the one from the Mormon Tabernacle. There were some real sweet older people in it, a lot of whom I grew to look up to because they were pillars in our little community.

There were even a couple who could sing.

But I sure thought they made a joyful noise. Page 96 in our Baptist hymnal was "At The Cross." A joyous hymn for believers, it was made even more joyous over the chorus. In the critical part of that chorus as they boomed out "At the cross, at the cross, where I first saw the light, and the burden of my heart rolled away," Brother Joe was in charge of singing the "rolled away" echo over the piano and organ. I can still hear it. It was one of the funniest things I have ever heard.

What made it even funnier is after the singing of the hymns, we in the youth department made bets on how long it would take Brother Joe to go to sleep in Brother Moore's sermon. And we aren't talking about any kind of sleep here. He and a few others would stay in the choir section behind our pastor, and Brother Joe would catch up on his REM sleep, mouth wide open.

For a fourteen-year-boy, this qualifies as high comedy.

It made for great community.

I have always had the good fortune to have at least one dear friend in every stage of my life. The kind of person who enjoys being around me typically has a sense of humor and also a very thick, tough skin, so he can take a joke on him, but he can dish it out, too.

There are few places where one enjoys more togetherness and community like that than on a baseball team. Once when I was sixteen I played on a team that was traveling to a tournament a few hours away. We kept winning, which meant we kept staying in a Howard Johnson's in a small town on the Tennessee-Alabama state line. Between games rain set in, which meant we had a lot of spare time on our hands. There were many things that happened in those hotel rooms, some of which were the funniest things I have ever witnessed—but wild horses can't drag most of them out of me now, and I think that would be a relief to some of the other guys.

One of the things I *will* share happened on one of those rain days. Our coaches were stir crazy and they went with a couple of the boys to the movies. Now what were they thinking? Leaving a dozen or so of us behind in a hotel all alone? I will never know. Having coached, I suspect they were at the point of "I either get out of here or I pluck each hair out of my head with tweezers one at a time."

Lo and behold, they left their door open to their room. One of our handiest team members decided to take a screwdriver, take their air vent off, and deposit some of his, ahem, "remains" that he collected in a cup. And turn the heat on.

The most important lesson I learned on that trip was to never let that guy in my house again.

In high school, the two guys I loved the most and I formed "the triangle." Our self-named little tribe was the foundation of many serious conversations and the place where the beginnings of manhood were first formed. Mike had quite a curious looking head so we aptly christened him "Squarehead," which he hated with a passion. Carey, the third leg in the triangle, got the moniker "Arnold Ziffel" after the pig on *Green Acres*. Mine was "Cowlick," for the big swoop at the front of my hair at the time.

I loved them, and they loved me. When I had my wreck, they showed me what real brotherhood looked like. All the trash talk we had done with each other went out the window, and they were by my bed telling me they loved me.

I knew they did, but hearing them say it showed me it was OK to say it. I had heard it all my life from my family, but this was different. They didn't love because they had to, because they were family, but because we shared a brotherhood.

You have already become acquainted with my friends Tracy and Gary through this book. Tracy is the golf pro at our local course, and Gary is a pretty good golfer. The golf association hosts a match play championship every year. One year, Gary and I both won our first six matches to get to the final, only to play each other. I had won the tournament against all odds (and I mean all odds—I am not that good) and was only beating my friend away from an extreme longshot repeat of my championship. Standing on the next to last hole, I was down by two holes. The best I could do was to win the last two holes and force a playoff. Faced with a twenty-foot putt to win the hole or lose the championship, I drained it. On the next hole, Gary looked glum. He didn't even finish the hole and we moved on to a playoff, where I won on the twenty-first hole.

Only after the match did he share why he was disappointed. He had already assumed he had won on the seventeenth hole and had prepared to shake my hand with a fart machine in his pocket and a set of redneck teeth in his mouth.

Yes, these are my friends.

Brotherhood, sisterhood, fellowship, community. My point in telling you about Brother Joe and his bellowing choruses, that little country church, poo in an air vent, beating Gary's tail, and the triangle of friendship is to make you smile and realize an important truth. In the smiling, you recall your friends, laughter, pranks, memories, and love. Those things have nothing to do with career success, winning golf tournaments (although, man, does *that* help give a person lifetime leverage with golf buddies) or acquiring things, power, or titles.

Choosing people, investing in others, and having them invest themselves in you—oh, man, does joy ever live in those places! As I think of stories, memories, and accomplishments in my life, the first things that come into my mind are—not things. They're people. Places. Memories. Sure, my work has given me joy and I have had the privilege of helping people—and for that, I am thankful. And I am thankful to have a reputation of helpfulness and integrity that I will strive to keep forever. But the people make my soul sing. Sharing the laughs, the tears, the fears, the insecurities, the love.

Our lives are made full by the people and the community we choose. All those hours we spend at the office? The plaques hanging on the wall? They mean nothing without your story. And what is your story now? Are you making those same memories now? Or are you too busy, just not enough time to get to it all?

I confess to you I lost my way on the road to real for a time. Life had me by the tail. It was spinning me around, and I was getting dizzy. I shoved everyone, every so-called distraction, out of my path so I could go, reap, claim, and grab what was mine in the world.

And I lost. I lost time that can never be replaced. I didn't take time-out for me. I got too busy to teach, to do the things that fed others, and in the process fed me, too.

I forgot that most paradoxical of lessons.

When we give to others, we receive more.

When we choose to close that truth off from ourselves, we surround ourselves with shallow relationships we call "friendships," but those bogus friendships are conditional on some thing, some circumstance. Change any of those, and those "relationships" are gone.

Alone, I am terrible. Surrounded, I feel alive. Giving, I know God's pleasure. Hoarding my time, myself, and my gifts, I am stifled, unable to really breathe. I teach primarily so I can be taught.

I could have died in that hospital in 1984. Without those friends and family who stood by me, I would never have lived. And there have been many since. Without them, I would dry up inside.

On the Road to Real

Who have you lost contact with that will always have a piece of your heart?

_____

Why did you lose contact with that person, and what can you do to rebuild that relationship?

_____

_____

On a scale of 1-10, with 1 being the least, how are you doing on spending dedicated time building and growing your relationships?

_____

How will you improve that?

_____

_____

CHAPTER 12

STRIVING OR LIVING?

Life is difficult.
> —Opening line in M. Scott Peck's *The Road Less Traveled*

It's not about you.
> —Opening line in Rick Warren's *Purpose-Driven Life*

WE ALL HAVE decisions to make on how we view the world. Because of upbringing, background and near-death, life-changing experience, I see the world differently than I did before. You have a similar process at work. You have been informed by the experiences you have had.

Perhaps to you, cornbread was a staple, and you don't like biscuits. In that sad case, I am not sure we can be friends. Or maybe you aren't a fan of my beloved Vols. There are just some things I'll never understand.

Maybe you are just tired. Life has beaten you down. Relationships in key areas of your life are a source of pain, aided by a river of regret that you don't know whether you can ever make it across.

What could the possibilities be for you?

Or do you choose to just not believe in them anymore?

Two great questions, but most of us refuse to dig below the surface of them, because we think the pain associated with digging ourselves out of the hole is greater than any benefit we might get from the experience. You begin to believe all the things that have been told to you. "It is impossible." "It is too hard." "You are too old." Really? Who says? "They" say that? Who are "they," anyway? Friends stuck in the same places as you?

If you believe what other people have to say about your future, stop for a minute. Take a long look at where these people are coming from and what they are. Are they true friends? Let me quote something from a modern version of a book that has a lot to say about friendship and love: "Love . . . always looks for the best, never looks back, but keeps going" (1 Cor. 13:7,THE MESSAGE). So let me ask again: Are the ones who are implanting this negativity in your mind the friends you really choose?

Or is the real enemy *you*? You and your poisoned way of thinking?

"Life is difficult." "It's not about you." Two of the greatest opening lines to books I have ever read. And they both ring true.

Is life difficult? I have laid out my story to you. It has been tough, and not what I would have chosen if I could have sat back at eighteen years old and designed my perfect future.

If we spent enough time together and you told me your story, I know I would hear the same for you. The charmed existence does not exist. We have bought it in movies, clinging to those images that fly by our eyes in stories that offer hope to those desperate for it. Things can really turn out OK, can't they? They did for Red Pollard (played by Tobey Maguire) in *Seabiscuit* (2003), right? And how about Andy Dufresne (Tim Robbins) in 1994's *The Shawshank Redemption*? Inspiring stories for sure. Yet in our desperation for the hope we cling to, we use standards that are impossible to meet. We buy into the standards the world has set for what happiness, success, having it all, is supposed to look like. We measure them up against our own lives, and we think we have failed.

And it's not about you. What do you do with that?

Most of us, selfish by nature, have been taught we are special. Reminds me of the time when I was a twelve-year-old pitcher and a fat, unathletic-looking kid came to the plate. I whispered to myself, "This guy is meat." Well now. . . the first pitch I threw him, he hit it into the next state. I guess my momma forgot to tell him I was special. . .

Did someone forget to tell the world that you are so "special" that the world owes you something? Without realizing it, we sometimes act as if everything in the world is ours for the taking.

We "special" people tell ourselves we're gonna get all we can while the gettin' is good. "I am gonna get mine." We think the first thing we must do is cut off a big slice of comfort to feed our hunger for it.

Your life is meant to be poured out for others. That is what is most important in our lives. Others need the hope your life can represent.

So we have some choices to make. Here's one choice:

So life is difficult, and it's not about me? Says who? It has always been about me. I have worked, I have *strived*, I have strained, to get to my goals. I thought this felt difficult, but I've discovered there is no light at the end of the tunnel because there will always be *new* roadblocks in our way to overcome. I know now that the life I had carved out for myself is not going to happen. It's a drag and a drain, but I gotta keep on. I gotta prove myself.

How's that working out for you?

The other outlook, the one with hope and truth attached to it, reads these things and says this:

OK. Life is difficult. I have seen that and know I will always be challenged in some area of my life, but it is also not all about me. And thank God for that. I have tried and tried to create the perfect world for myself and I am tired. I want to get outside myself and be a better friend, son or daughter, parent, spouse. I want to love others, and to do that genuinely, I have to get outside of always thinking about myself.

All this striving and straining. Hard work is a virtue, to be sure, in balance.

But some things have been discovered. We all enjoy money and we all want more of it. That is a goal that is pretty universal. We aren't sure entirely what we would do with it, or even if we could handle it properly if given the circumstance. But we want our shot at it. For those who have money and thought it would fill the hole for you, you have discovered what I have seen in my own life and my clients. Money, as your sole end, will let you down. It will go away, or it will create more problems than you ever envisioned. As J. Paul Getty once allegedly said, "Money won't make you happy, but it will sure keep your kids close to you." Funny words spoken from a man who knew.

We chase careers and titles hoping those will make us feel superior and important—that somehow that power will be the salve we seek for our soul. Yet I have seen and experienced that those things alone have little meaning when not balanced by what we truly desire.

We work to create the perfect marriage only to find we have married someone with faults, sometimes as big as our own. How dare they! Your significant other can no more plug the hole in you by themselves than I have a future as a Speedo® model.

At 2009's Super Bowl, Bruce Springsteen was the halftime entertainment. A friend pointed out his opening line as being the question we all really want someone to scream at us.

"Is anyone alive out there?"

I went through years of just plugging ahead, looking for my next move, my questions mostly starting with "How do I get to this goal?," or "that goal? ," or "next year's goal?" I blew obstacles to the side, ignored any warnings of others, and dove headfirst into getting what I wanted. I. What *I* wanted. Not the effects on others, not in some great design of my life, but as mindlessly as a dog chases a pork chop, never thinking he might choke to death on the bone.

But I wasn't alive. I was young and full of energy, and my colleagues at work would remind me and my clients about all the talent

I possessed—that I was a rising star—and my titles and credentials hanging tastefully on my office wall would impress them. I had a great looking family and had stayed married. Isn't that enough?

One small problem presented itself over time, though. Why was I doing all this? Many years would go by before I would enter into the process I speak of now.

You have heard it said that "life begins at forty," when the last child leaves the house and the dog dies, all that.

I say life begins when you say it does.

There exists in our life a great blank. That's spelled "b–l–a–n–k." Walk with me for a bit here.

Paul was the original author of this statement in Philippians 1:21: "For to me, to live is <u>Christ</u>." He had his blank filled in.

What is it you are living for? What is your purpose, the reason you are here, the impact you want to have? In other words, examine your life for a moment and fill in the blank. It looks like this: My life is about_____.

We mostly live without that singleminded purpose that makes life worth living. We have allowed ourselves to be stretched—pulled—and demanded of, in so many ways.

What is it you are giving your life to? Money? Power? Control? Fame? Materialism? Sex?

How's that working out for you?

Make no mistake about it. You *are* giving yourself to some cause, or person. *Not* filling in the blank is not an option for those who wish to live. Not filling in the blank is to cast a vote for more of the same, to live in the clouds of busyness and activity, without being conscious and aware of what you will give yourself to.

Now. Once you have filled in the blank, ask yourself: Is this worth giving my life to?

We all set out with noble causes. Yes, we want money and security, and for some the toys of life are the initial drivers in our youthful charging ahead. But who consciously fills in their blank with those things? Most people I have talked to would instead give the "beauty pageant" answer: We want to be about others, help those less fortunate, raise great kids, leave a strong legacy.

Yet when we line up what we are *doing* versus what we are supposed to be *about*, the two simply don't meet up.

As an aside, given the brutally tough times we are going through collectively during the writing of this book—a stock market on a downward spiral, prices of all our stuff we have run after for so long dropping through the floor and many hard-working people not being able to pay their mortgages—is this not *exactly* the time to be having a little self-examination in this area?

In our striving, we do a lot of daydreaming as we find that all that strain we put on ourselves in order to get to our destination is pulling us further and further away from the very dream that our running is supposed to get us to.

Maybe you've seen this story somewhere. I don't know where it originally comes from, but I read it recently in, of all places, a sandwich shop. It illustrates what I'm trying to say in an unforgettable way:

> An American businessman was at the pier of a small coastal Mexican village when a small boat with just one fisherman docked. Inside the small boat were several large yellow-fin tuna. The American complimented the Mexican on the quality of his fish and asked how long it took to catch them. The Mexican replied, "Only a little while." The American then asked why didn't he stay out longer and catch more fish. The Mexican said he had enough to support his family's immediate needs. The American then asked, "But what do you do with the rest of your time?
>
> The Mexican fisherman said, "I sleep late, fish a little, play with my children, take siesta with my wife, Maria, stroll into the village each evening where I sip wine and play guitar with my amigos. I have a full and busy life, Senor.
>
> The American scoffed, "I am a Harvard MBA and could help you. You should spend more time fishing, and with the proceeds buy a bigger boat, and with the proceeds from the bigger boat you could buy several boats, and eventually you would have a fleet of fishing boats. Instead of selling your catch to a middleman you would sell directly to the processor, eventually opening your own cannery. You would control the product, processing and distribution. You would need to leave this small coastal fishing

village and move to Mexico City, then Los Angeles and eventually New York City where you will run your expanding enterprise."

The Mexican fisherman asked, "But Señor, how long will this all take?" To which the American replied, "Fifteen to twenty years."

"But what then, Señor?"

The American laughed and said, "That's the best part. When the time is right you would announce an IPO and sell your company stock to the public and become very rich. You would make millions."

"Millions, Señor? Then what?"

The American said, "Then you would retire. Move to a small coastal fishing village where you would sleep late, fish a little, play with your kids, take siesta with your wife, stroll to the village in the evenings where you could sip wine and play your guitar with your amigos."

Might you have everything you need right in front of you?

I certainly have been known to make it awfully tough on myself. One such time came on a business trip for a week of executive education at the Wharton School of Business at the University of Pennsylvania. It was the second year in a three-year program, and even though it was one of the most phenomenal professional experiences I have ever had, I dreaded the week away from my family, complained of traveling, going to the cold weather, being away from my family, blah blah blah, whatever. A real complaint bucket.

One year, I got there and it immediately reminded me of why I had made it a priority to take the time away. High learning, meeting a cultural mix of people you simply cannot find in middle Tennessee, having time to think and reflect, just a wonderful time.

One day in particular was instructive as to how I, and by default, we, can get off track. A sports fan, I had bought tickets for an Ivy League basketball game in the great old arena, the Palestra. I was excited, and had bought enough for some friends to join up with me. The day of the game, I took our lunch break to walk across campus to pick up the tickets.

The tickets were waiting for me at Will Call just like I had requested. Great. It was a rare beautiful day out, and I took the time to walk on parts of the beautiful campus I had not seen. The morning had been full of promise with spot-on instruction in my business, and I had connected with some people I was looking forward to getting to know better after our classes departed.

I called my wife on my walk and told her what a good day it had been, the walk, the people, all of it. I could hear the excitement in my own voice. Joy and fulfillment were in my heart.

As I went to my next class assignment, I discovered I did not have the tickets. They were gone. I began to take my seat, knowing I had to do something. Knowing myself like I do, I knew I had to get out of there and address the situation immediately. People were counting on me! I couldn't let them down. I was in charge of the tickets!

Now notice something. I had the best possible day going at that place in time. And then old demons came and whispered in my ear.

Notice—I was on a high, and the enemy attacked, my saboteur, if you will. How stupid am I? I walked into my class and could not get it off my mind. Knowing myself as I do, I wouldn't have heard a word the professor said. So I headed back out *again* on a 35-minute round trip walk. It didn't even hit me that my legs felt great—and that's not always the case with those scarred, pinned, creaky reminders of when I was eighteen.

I walked back, flogging myself, not noticing the beauty of the campus this time, all the while making up things I could tell the ticket office guy, knowing if I didn't lie my way out of it, I would have to buy four more tickets.

I began making up stories: I threw them away at lunch when I was finished. I was mugged. A kid pointed a water pistol at me and I peed my pants. They blew into a storm drain.

I did not trust God.

When I walked into the ticket office, the guy's look told me he remembered me. I walked to the window and said, "I have been thinking up lies all the way back over here, but here is the deal. I lost the tickets I picked up about an hour ago."

He looked back at me, smiled, and said, "OK. I will reprint them for you."

I felt like a fool. All the way back, I laughed at myself. Simple truth delivered me out of a pretty minor situation. But how major had I made it?

We do this all the time. Take minor things and turn them into acts of war. War in our own brains. And we do not trust that something bigger is at work.

Now I ask you. Whatever that brilliant professor had to say that I was so grieved to miss for an hour, would it have instructed me as much as what I learned about telling the truth did? I doubt it. I like that lesson as much as anything I have ever been taught by another human being.

As I spoke recently with Bruce Albert, a fantastic consultant from Boston, he made a comment to me that struck at the heart of this matter. He told me he had always encouraged his children to follow this basic tenet:

> You always achieve highest when you are doing the thing that you love. When you are not operating in your passion, the smallest obstacles can seem like enormous roadblocks to you. And the money is never enough. But when you are doing that which you love, the roadblocks just become part of the deal. You can withstand those things easily because it's just part of it, and because it just leads to getting to be at your love.

I spent some time with a friend of mine recently, and the subject of what drives us came up. He is a very successful businessman with his own financial services firm and employs more than a hundred people. As a result, his life is chaotic. On a face to face visit to meet with his leadership coach, he mentioned to him how he might want to simplify and do some consulting so he could leave the hectic life behind him. His coach scoffed at the idea and told him, "You can't. You are addicted to the 'green sheets.'"

The green sheets are weekly report cards that show him exactly where he stands in every category imaginable against his competition. What he told me next was one of those jaw-dropping pieces of wisdom you can only get by surrounding yourself with good people whom you know fully.

"Steve, I realized he was right. As bad as that may sound, it is what drives me. I want to beat my competitors." It is the thing that got his blood flowing and got him out of bed every morning.

Here is the magic, and it has two pieces. He knew what drove him, and he had someone else in his life to reinforce what he knew, but needed to hear.

We cannot do it alone.

Ultimately what drives the goal of my friend is helping those choosing a career in his firm to be successful. The result, the end game, is the thing he takes pride in, but his charge comes from seeing people succeed. If he set out to slash and burn, taking no prisoners, what kind of success would he have? Temporary perhaps, but nothing as lasting as what he has built.

What is your passion? My friend had figured out what drove him, what inspired him. It may not be your story, but we can define our passions. They generally look like this:

- You would do it for nothing.
- You want to share it with others.
- It brings you joy.
- It gives you energy.

It's not about us. Oh, at the end of it all we get our reward, but the process of seeing others enriched by our attention and gifts is where life lays in front of us. Going to bed having helped someone make himself or herself better and along the way having our own souls fed—that is where the full life exists. As long as it is about you, or me, it will be empty. Maybe not today, but we will find ourselves leaning against the wall of our soul knowing we are wasting on ourselves what was meant to be given away.

So what are your green sheets? What gets your blood flowing? Do you feel the smallest of obstacles getting in your way? Are you making mountains out of molehills?

What do you not just love, but it stirs your soul? Spend your life doing that thing, and as Pedro said in *Napoleon Dynamite* (2004), "Vote for me and all your wildest dreams will come true." (*Napoleon Dynamite* being one of the top films ever made—but everyone already knows that, right?

Choose the other, the stuck place, and no amount of money, titles, and prestige can rub the place that hurts.

Are you just tired? I mean the kind of tired that exists in a place sleep won't touch. Just tired.

Our souls cry to be fed. Life is difficult. And it's not about you. And thank God for it.

What will you decide?

Real living awaits your decision.

Are you alive out there?

On the Road to Real

What moves your soul? What is that thing that when you are at it, you say, "Ah, this is it. This is where I feel alive?"

_____

What activity, goal, or purpose are you giving your life to?

_____

Is that thing what you set out to be about? _____

If not, what can you do about that?

_____

_____

How long will you allow yourself to be a slave to the things that *don't* make you come alive?

CHAPTER 13

SO NOW WHAT?

Never under any circumstances take a laxative and a sleeping aid at the same time.

—Dave Barry

Get busy living or get busy dying.
— Red (Morgan Freeman) in *Shawshank Redemption*

SOME THINGS YOU only learn from experience.
I had to learn the hard way that gum will really stick to your hair, and that it is not a good idea to take a pair of scissors and cut the gum out at the root. I spent a month looking like I was Alfalfa from "The Little Rascals" when I was in the third grade.

Evil Knievel was all the rage when I was a kid. I watched one of his jumps one day on *ABC's Wide World of Sports* and, inspired, promptly went behind my Pop's tool shed and found a large tree branch and a sheet of plywood and made myself a ramp. Launch angles, speed, and such details never crossed my mind. With a full head of steam, I went approximately 1400 feet in the air before nearly impaling myself on the tree branch I had anchored in the ground as the plywood slipped away.

Note to self: Cross physics off as a career alternative.

Here are some other things I have learned:

- It takes a lot of time to pour oil into your car when you pour it down the dipstick hole.
- When you cake peanut butter under someone's car door handle, it takes weeks to get it all cleaned off when you find a nice glob of it under your own.
- When you get your tonsils out, you can have all the ice cream you want. They don't tell you eating it will be like eating shards of glass. Deceivers!
- Having a Shrek-sized head means never turning down a hat you try on if, by some stroke of luck, it actually fits your head.
- Never drink a full bottle of water before going in front of a crowd for a sixty-minute presentation.
- When you park your car for a few hours with the sunroof open and a hailstorm comes, it is not cool.

I've learned some other things, too. Some of them about kids, some of them serious, others pretty funny—well, after the fact, anyway:

- Talk up a road trip until the kids can't wait for the ride and then wait five minutes after getting in the car for one of them to say, "How much more longer?" or "Are we there yet?"
- When a Teenager is trying to convince you to give in about something and the arguments sound familiar, it's because they are—you used the same ones on your parents.
- To an adolescent, there is nothing in the world more embarrassing than a parent. (OK, I borrowed that one from Dave Barry.)
- A kid is guaranteed to disappoint you at one point or another, because he or she is a kid.
- A kid is guaranteed to let you down at one point or another, because he or she is just like you.

Here's the biggest one: Kids are the ultimate catch-and-release program. The release date comes on you before you know it. It is inevitable, and that's the way it should be.

Other kinds of experiences inform us, too. People who have failed financially have a hard time taking any risk that will put them back in that spot ever again. Failed relationships build walls around us, because we fear being hurt again. A business fails and we believe our dreams are gone, never to take flight again. The big chance passed us by, never to be realized.

Mostly, we avoid pain that we know.

As we grow a little older, we will do whatever is necessary to avoid pain. We retreat to safe places, to seek out our own comfort.

Experience can be a wonderful thing. We fought for it, paid for it, and earned it. Wisdom springs from the things we have endured.

I want to propose one final question to you, though.

What if the very best of your life
lies directly in front of you?

Or, is the end game for you to be sitting on some beach somewhere, sipping drinks with little umbrellas in them, staring into the distance, and patting yourself on the back while trying to convince yourself about how good you were?

Sadly, my friend Steve just lost his best friend since the first grade in a freak accident. As he talked with me about his loss, he made a haunting, profound, and true statement. "We just don't have much time left. We think we do, but the truth is, we just don't have much time left."

In grief and shock, Steve was facing his mortality, and some really tough truth was smacking him in the face. At fifty-five, he has gained wisdom and perspective that only experience can teach. What flew at me was that the statement is true for all of us, regardless of age or experience.

I could have, and perhaps by all reason should have, died in my car accident. I was forced at an early age to realize how quickly we could be gone. But I haven't always treated my life in a precious way even when armed with that knowledge. I lost a good friend a few years back after talking with him about a golf game we scheduled for later in the week. He went into a coma that very night and passed away five days later. Seeing his family deal with the aftermath was a haunting experience that brought this close to home all over again and on another level.

When we are teenagers, we are invincible. When college is over, we begin those careers, start having families, and begin our journey into adulthood with goals in mind, but with short-term sighting and without earned experience.

"We don't have much time."

So what do you do with that?

That knowledge forces me to *action*. It makes me want to get serious about my passions—intentionally—right now. I want to clear my life of those things that are not in line with my passions and begin being about those things, those permanent things, that will stay behind after I am gone. People, relationship, memories that bring joy and laughter, impact. A legacy.

Age does not determine a legacy. Your actions do.

There is no end. The finish line is a mirage of our minds. We don't even finish when we quit breathing, for all the impact you have had in others' lives on, and it and shapes and forms all the people they come into contact with. More than a piece of you lives on.

In the movie *The Bucket List* (2007), Jack Nicholson plays Edward Cole, a man who has pretty well slashed and burned through his life, creating a financial fortune, but who is bankrupt in his joy and in his relationships. When he gets cancer, he encounters Carter Chambers, a blue-collar worker played by Morgan Freeman who has been stricken by cancer, as well.

After a time when their differences are apparent, the men find a common bond and decide to embark on a trip to accomplish and see all the things they want to see and experience before they die, forming "the bucket list"—things they want to do before they "kick the bucket."

Two things said as the movie comes to a close give me a glimpse of what our future can hold.

Sitting atop the Great Pyramids, after Chambers has shared some wisdom, Cole looks at him and says, "I wish I had met you before we were dead." Isn't it funny that a man who had stepped out of his normal comfort zone and gotten to know someone he would have been too busy to even notice before sickness began to claim him, ends up realizing the value in relationship?

Enter into real relationships. I will end my life with some things I would like to do over. Building meaningful relationships will not be on that list.

Cole also says something else, when he speaks at his friend's funeral. At age eighty, he says, "The last three months of his life were the best of mine."

The best lies ahead for you, but you have to choose it. It will not come and find you. This is not some spectator sport. You are in charge. Don't retreat in fear, give in to bitterness, or get small and slowly go away because you *think* your big chance slipped away.

Toward the end of *The Legend of Bagger Vance*, Junuh has been going along quite nicely, only to sabotage himself by allowing his old demons to get hold of him. He is gripped with his old fears, forgetting the new message he is learning and that has him on the edge of winning his match against huge odds, when he finds himself in the woods and is overwhelmed by his haunting.

Bagger lays out the ultimate choice we all face.

> "Time for you to come on out the shadows.
> Time for you to choose."

Past or today? Bad experiences versus the hope tomorrow brings? Wallowing in your pain and sorrow or authoring a fresh ending? Continue to not be fully known, and never experience the freedom that awaits?

I have been Junuh. Scared to come out the shadows. Afraid to show up big. Afraid I wasn't enough.

Have you?

Tell the truth about yourself and the world around you. Engage head-on into loving people. Choose community. Take the fork in the road.

And so, I give you hope.

What would you do if you were not afraid?

For far too much of my life, fear gripped me and I chose the safe way. I chose the path of what I thought was survival. When I had my wreck, I buried all my angst, swallowed hard, and kept it to myself. I went down the path of destruction early in college, only to be forced out of it by my new wife, never stopping to ask myself why I hurt so much, for fear I would have to deal with the answer, that it would all bubble to the surface—and I couldn't have that. First kid on the way? Work like there is no tomorrow. Second kid? Work even harder.

Then when my business failed and bankruptcy loomed, my work life was ruled by fear for a long time. In total brokenness I climbed out of the hole and built a successful practice, and slowly I realized that one thing I could do that gave my work life some purpose was to help other people realize their dreams. I loved that aspect, and I believed I had been helpful.

But. . .there was still the matter of myself to deal with. I had not yet found the fullness of my calling in life. I had not yet found my joy. Vicki and I would talk about whether or not we were happy in our lives, and we would respond with all the blessings in our life, list the reasons we were happy, as though we were selling the idea to one another. When we peeled back the layers, we realized that, yes, we had love, material things, our needs were provided for, and our health. That is enough, isn't it?

Until we both realized there was one important element missing. Our lives were missing joy. The blessings may be enough for some, but we decided to seek joy.

For me, joy is that thing that lets us know we are on the right path, of living my God-given purpose out. I had survived and settled, but I knew that my heart was not full. Joy is a requirement.

What that means for me is living the purpose that God set in my heart. Here again are my criteria:

- I would do it for nothing.
- I have to share it with others.
- It brings me joy.
- It gives me energy.

I am not talking about I-just-won-the-lottery joy. I am talking about my heart being full with what I do, to know my work is deeply impacting others, to know—just *know*—that the very reason for my being placed here is being lifted up in what I do and who I am. One of the things we discovered and noticed in other people's lives whom we admired was that one thing they all had in common was they did not retreat to some safe, comfortable place. They *shared* their lives with others. It simply was not all about them, as much as we buy that pie-in-the–sky thinking.

Surviving and settling. I had done it long enough. Fear would not rule me any longer. I decided to step out, go against a lot of conventional ways of thinking, and be totally sold out to the idea of being true to who I am. And so I chased my dreams.

We all have these moments, but so many of us choose to ignore them due to our mortal fear of change. For those who lift up their heads, take the risk, and enter the chase, the story sounds familiar—and exciting.

In one enormous plant we have in my community, people make a better living than they ever thought they would. It comes at a good deal of expense to them personally. The job is difficult, and the culture is hard-charging and relentless. Recently, the company offered a buyout package and several came to me for advice. Of the ones I know that have left, outside the relationships they had there, they do not miss it. One man spoke a deep truth to me.

"Once I got outside the plant, I realized how little life I had. How big the world was and how small I had made it. I didn't realize the opportunities that existed for me. I have never felt better in my life."

Is your story similar? Are you ready to lift your head and see what the world has for you?

I tell you what I did. *I said, "Enough. I am ready to design what lays ahead for me for the first time in my life."* It only took a little more than 40 years.

Should you?

Employ a coach. Get a mentor. Mentor someone else. Give. Receive. Get still. Get simple.

As a result of stopping, I have more opportunities than ever in my life. The world has opened up to me. Speaking, teaching, and coaching had long been my passion. I decided to reach out to hug that dream, and it hugged back.

I also have my sanity back. My son Ben and I are only going to eight parks in four days this summer. (Relax. I joke.)

Do it not only for yourself. Do it for those who love you. They want you back.

A friend of mine who is in the music business has spent a good deal of his life on the road. Sensing a need to be with a family of four children, he and his wife decided he should take a job at my church that had been offered to him that would keep him at home. The timing was incredible, as his wonderful wife was stricken with cancer shortly thereafter.

Thankfully, the story has a happy follow-up. His wife, after a serious battle, is in remission and is cancer free. A fantastic opportunity came up for him to rejoin a band and go back on the road, and he struggled with the size and implications of his decision.

A conversation with one of his children helped make the decision much simpler. His son told him, "Go. Take it. When you were on the road before, I really got more of you then. When you were home, you were *home*. Now that you are here all the time, I get less of you because you aren't really *here* as much."

I have spent a lot of time with my family, and don't regret a minute of it. (Well, there is one time. That time in the car while my daughter was yawning in Technicolor, blowing chunks, that was no good.)

But the moments that are special to me are the moments where I was really, really *there* with them, and I am afraid they have been too few. Perhaps our best Christmas happened one year after I realized what I really wanted to give my family for Christmas was time together. I decided that all logical criteria would fly out the window and wrapped for each one in my family a gift that was a hint of what I was giving them. We were going to Maui, our number one destination we had talked about collectively several times. As they opened their gifts, I danced in singing Don Ho-style while wearing a grass skirt. The ensuing electric shock therapy seems to have cleared my kids from that scarring sight.

That day, and on that trip, man, I was *there* with them. It really would not have mattered where we were—they had all of me. I dropped *all* my cares and really showed up. Sure, the time we spent was in a Garden of Eden place, and it cost roughly the GDP of Lithuania. But being together and away from "stuff" gave us time to really *be* there. That trip will forever remain as one of the precious memories I wanted so much to engrave in my kids' minds.

In fact, that trip awakened me to a lot of the truths that I have written about here. One morning, I got up early and walked down to the beach and saw something that struck close to home and made me want to shape my life. A simple thing, but profound. There were people *everywhere* on their cell phones and BlackBerry devices conducting business. In one of the most beautiful places in the world. As the sun came up. And I noticed that they didn't even see it.

Look, I get it. No judgment here. I just choose not to live that way. I wanted to stay right there and give my family . . . me. The real me, not some piece of me that is left after I give the office my approval and orders and get distracted.

And those two weeks I was gone? The world seemed to spin just fine without me involved.

Get quiet. Get still. Say no, and get ready for the Big Yes. Instead of saying OK, followed by a heavy sigh, get ready to enter into your Yes with passion.

Love while you still have the chance.

Follow your passion. God placed it there for your enjoyment. And others are starving for it.

Quit asking, "How much more longer?"

Be present.

Tell the truth, especially when it hurts.

Come on out of the shadows.

Choose.

ACKNOWLEDGMENTS

WRITING MY STORY has shown me that the importance I place on telling the truth comes from a long line of family that cared about such things. I would be remiss to not acknowledge my parents, Felton and Peggy Elder and my sister Sandy, along with a long line of past generations, about whom I was vastly educated growing up. Protecting the family name was serious business. We had and have our warts, but I learned truly what a family looked like early on. Obviously, I cannot thank them or my grandparents, my Mammie and Pop, enough for what they gave me. Protecting that legacy is now my joyful duty.

I never really knew my great-grandfather, but Granny Elder was alive and kicking well into my teens. It is only as I grow older that I truly appreciate both, for what they stood for. Family was their first, and really only, concern. In what we call "a simpler time," the truth of it is that they raised eleven children during and throughout the Depression, doing what they had to do to survive. My Pop was the third of six sons, joining five daughters. They served in wars, died in industrial accidents, and had their ups and downs, but they were the epitome of family. They modeled to a young boy how to love, protect, and provide, not necessarily with material things, but to give love, support, and precious memories through family traditions. They are gone now, but I thank them for the Elder name and the honor of carrying it forward.

When one endeavors to do such a thing as the writing of this book, as with anything we take on bigger than ourselves, there is a price to be paid. My wife Vicki has had to listen to me flesh these thoughts out, which I assure you is one of the tougher things she has involuntarily taken on during our twenty-one years together.

My children are the main motivating force behind this book. It is my small contribution to their lives that I show them a father who doesn't simply talk at them, but has tried in the middle of the challenges all parents face to be true and authentic. A father has no greater joy than to see his children grow from their mistakes and triumphs alike, and to share them fully with the people who love you most and unconditionally.

My coach, Irene Gardiner-Harding, has been a godsend. A person who deeply "gets it," and with whom you can objectively examine the truth of your life, is a great gift. She has lifted me in ways that I can never fully repay her for.

Finally, to all my buddies and colleagues, those who have forged friendships with me over the years, those who have along with me shared the tears, the laughter, and the uncomfortable but freeing truth sessions, I love you all. The list is too long to name everyone, but I have to thank Gary, Tracy, and later, John for being the guys with whom I first walked into the truth. Without you and the time we have spent together, I shudder to think how my life would have ended up and where I would be now.

Community has lifted me, family has loved me, Jesus saved me, and the truth set me free. I am a far richer man than I ever set out to be. I just didn't know what true wealth was for a while, but I have it in more than a good measure.

I wish you this kind of wealth.

ABOUT THE AUTHOR

STEVE ELDER IS a keynote speaker and a coach who works with individuals and corporate teams. He draws on personal and professional experiences from twenty years in the financial services industry to challenge those he works with to begin living life in earnest, with passion, and to see life through a different lens.

A graduate of the University of Tennessee, Steve live in Murfreesboro, TN with his wife and two teenage children. *How Much More Longer* is his first book. For more information, please see www.elderspeaks.com

PW

LaVergne, TN USA
12 July 2010
189193LV00004B/70/P